THE PROFESSIONAL ACTOR

FROM AUDITION TO PERFORMANCE

THE
PROFESSIONAL
ACTOR
FROM AUDITION TO PERFORMANCE

Tom Markus

DRAMA BOOK SPECIALISTS (Publishers) *New York*

Copyright © 1979 by Tom Markus

FIRST EDITION

All rights reserved under the International and Pan-American
Copyright Conventions. For information address
Drama Book Specialists (Publishers),
150 West 52nd Street, New York, New York 10019.

Library of Congress Cataloging in Publication Data

Markus, Tom.
 The professional actor—from audition to
performance.

 1. Acting—Vocational guidance. I. Title.

PN2055.M27 792'.028'023 79-16668

ISBN 0-910482-91-8
ISBN 0-89676-009-X pbk.

10 9 8 7 6 5 4 3 2 9 0 1 1 2 2 3 3 4 4 5 5 6 6 7 7 8 8 9

Manufactured in the United States of America

CONTENTS

Preface 3

Prologue 5

Auditions 21

Rehearsals 49

Performances 133

Between Engagements 161

PREFACE

To write a book is to hope someone will read it. Or at least buy it and put it on a shelf in preparation for that dreary day when nothing will serve but to pull it down, crack its spine, and test its mettle. And so, dear actor, permit me to guide your hand until your eye is ready and to direct you where to place this book upon your shelf. Place it snugly between Robert Cohen's *Acting Professionally* and Michael Green's *The Art of Coarse Acting*. Between the fire and earth of a sensible handbook and the bubbly breath of Mr. Green's wit. Beyond those trusty flanks, in casual disarray, I would be flattered to learn you'd placed William Goldman's *The Season*, William Gibson's *The Seasaw Log*, J.D. Salinger's *Franny and Zooey*, William Redfield's *Letters From An Actor*, Arthur Cantor's *The Playmakers*, and close by—but not so near as to invite corruption—Stanislavsky's *An Actor Prepares*.

To write a book is to reveal an indebtedness to more people

3

than a preface can in reason honor. To those whose names should be here but are not, my apologies. I hope you know who you are, as I may appear to have unjustly included you only in this general thanks to all those teachers who have taught me and all those students I have taught; to all those directors I have acted for and all those actors I've directed. Yet certain names cannot be dispatched so cavalierly, and I wish to extend particular appreciation to Monroe Lippman, who must live with the knowledge that he started me in this business; Paul Hostetler for continuing me along that path; Bob Corrigan for teaching me to think hard, if deviously; Bernie Dukore for trying to teach me to think straight; Wal Cherry for his hospitality and encouragement during the writing; Chuck Sachs for always taking time from his imminent career to listen to my dreams; Gordon Heath for teaching me to love the theatre; Bob Potter for appearing to believe I'm as good as I tell him I am; and Mike Addison who, with unerring accuracy and desired frequency, hits me right in the *hubris* with a pig's bladder.

And finally my sincere bow to my mother, my father, and my son Lindsay.

PROLOGUE

"I'm going to have to let him go."

"What did he do?"

"I won't keep him. He's got to go."

"But what does he do?"

"He disrupts rehearsals. He talks all the damn time. He thinks he's too good to play anything but leads. He wants to run before he can crawl."

"Well, it's your own fault. Your shouldn't have given him a lead in the *Shrew*. I never found him difficult."

"No, no. He wastes time and he's impossible. No, I'm going to let him go."

This conversation took place between the general manager of a major professional theatre and the head of an important acting conservatory. I've left out the names, to protect all concerned. The subject was a recent graduate of the conservatory and it was evident to me, by the end of the conversation which went on longer than the brief exchange recorded here, that a young actor was likely to be fired. Not because he couldn't act, but because he couldn't behave as an actor.

That same conversation goes on around the world all the time. Young (and not so young) actors lose jobs or fail to get jobs because they don't know the rules for the profession they follow. They may be wonderfully talented and they may have received formidable training in the craft of their profession. But somehow they have not acquired the knowledge they need to work in the profession. Annually, in the United States and elsewhere, acting students leave training institutions, private coaches, or amateur theatre groups and descend on the casting centers of their respective countries seeking work. And they have talent, many of them. But without correct work habits and without a sound knowledge of professional behavior their chances of employment are seriously reduced. There is fierce competition for jobs in the theatre and employers don't have to waste their time on actors who can't "cut it." Like the young actor above, they're going to be "let go."

This book is a handbook, a beginner's guide to professional behavior for the actor. I hope it will provide neophyte and veteran alike with some guidelines toward professional attitudes and work habits. Now, don't expect to get work just because you've read and assimilated the notions in the pages that follow. No book can do that for you: not your how-to-act text nor your how-to-get-an-acting-job text. All this modest book can provide you with are some ways you can do your job effectively—some ways to become employable—some ways to keep a job if you're lucky enough to get one—some ways to help yourself get hired again, once a job is completed.

Definitions

A first area of concern, one we'd best deal with before going any further, is a matter of definitions: actor, artist, performer, talent. What precisely is this thing you think you are? If you're working a television show, you'll hear yourself referred to as the "talent." In the souvenir program of a permanent theatre company, you may find your picture and bio under a category called "artists." When you are denied a lease on an apartment, you may discover it is because you are that irresponsible and untrustworthy thing called an "actor."

The _Webster's Third New International Dictionary_ gives a good starting place: "a theatrical performer; someone that acts in a stage play, motion picture, radio or television play, or a dramatic sketch." With provocative bias, _Webster's_ defines an actress as "a woman who takes part in any affair; a female actor." I won't comment on the first part of that definition, except to observe that it may be just such notions which led Englishman George Moore to remark that "acting is therefore the lowest of the arts, if it is an art at all."

Is an actor an artist? Only if he has created a work of art, something that exists outside the artist and independent of him. It is something which the deliberate and intentioned application of his craft or skill has brought into existence—something which communicates both delight and instruction. An audience must be pleased and edified before an actor can be said to have created a work of art, can be called an artist. I would say that Paul Scofield's performance as King Lear was a work of art, and therefore I may call him an artist. So too is Lord Olivier, for his creations of many roles, notably Othello, Archie Rice, Shylock, James Tyrone. So too is Marlon Brando, for his work on stage and film in such shows as _A Streetcar Named Desire, Last Tango in Paris,_ and _The Teahouse of the August Moon._ So too is Jessica Tandy, for her performances in such works as _A Delicate Balance, Not I,_ and _The Gin Game._

The list of artists is very long. Scofield, Olivier, Tandy, Brando, and hundreds of others may be called artists because they have created works of art. But "artist" is not a label an actor may place upon himself; it is not something one puts on a passport in the blank space for profession. It is a label others give you, if and when you merit it, if and when you use your skills to communicate some instructive revelation which delights an audience, if and when you create a work of art. Let us, now and henceforth, relinquish discussions of actors as artists, and return to considering what it is that an actor is and does.

Acting, wrote Alexander Bakshy early in this century, "is the effort to appear different to what one really is; it is the practice of make-believe. In life we exercise this faculty of complete or partial disguise in order to achieve a variety of practical ends;

some innocent, some sinister, some serious, some jocular." In life we act, then. And on stage, an actor is one who uses this particular human faculty in a pre-planned pattern to contribute to a fiction which intends to delight and instruct us, the audience. The degree of each actor's effectiveness is arguable, and there are many opinions as to what is good and bad acting. George Burns, shortly before receiving an Academy Award for his performance in the film of Neil Simon's *The Sunshine Boys*, put it this way: "Good acting is when Walter Matthau says to me 'How are you?' and I answer 'Fine.' That's good acting. If Walter Matthau asks me 'How are you?' and I answer 'I think it fell on the floor' then that's bad acting." But, wit apart, we must deal with acting in its simplest terms, and return to *Webster's Third New International* to discover that acting is "the art or practice of representing a character on the stage or in a motion picture or radio or television play." If you do that, for the purposes of the pages that follow, you are an actor. You may or may not have talent; you may or may not be an artist. But you surely are an actor, and as an actor, you need to know how to behave.

You're an actor only once you've been engaged to act. You're a professional actor only once you're being remunerated for your time—whether that is as a card-carrying member of one of the theatrical unions or as a member of an acting commune that receives its recompense in eggs and grain from its appreciative audiences. Most of the remarks in this book will be aimed at the conventional, commercial theatre as it is practiced in the English-speaking world. As an American, most familiar with the theatre in America, my observations will have a national bias. But as I've traveled and worked in England, Canada, and Australia, I have found no essential differences, and I am hopeful that the body of this work will be widely applicable. So: what does it take to become a professional actor? I believe there are five requisites I can identify, and each is worthy of some discussion. They are *talent, training, luck, contacts, employability*. Let's look at each in turn.

Five Requisites For A Professional Actor

TALENT   The world is crawling with it. The number of actors in London, New York, Sydney, and Toronto who have talent is astonishing. The number of talented young actors and would-be actors going through training institutions annually is astounding. The number of people in non-theatrical professions who have theatrical talent is overwhelming. Talent, simply, is that inexplicable quality many people have which makes other people want to know about them, watch them, listen to them. It's easy to identify, but tough to define. Nor need we define it. People will tell you if you have it: by casting you in roles, or seeking your company, or heeding your opinions. In the theatre it is easy to identify. Go see a large-cast play or a musical with a chorus of singers and dancers. See them all dressed essentially alike, involved in the same piece of choreography, or carrying the same spears. Which one do you look at? That's the one with talent. As an actor you won't get beyond the chorus or the crowd of extras without it, no matter how you develop your skills, so it will be evident to you early in your career whether or not you have talent. You'll be plucked from the army and given that unenviable line, "The Queen, my lord, is dead." Or you'll find yourself singing a short solo, even though the girl beside you has a purer voice. But be careful. When you discover that you have talent, that there is something about you which others find interesting, you are likely to get a fat head, likely to assume falsely that henceforth the world should note you well and reward you for being yourself. Well, get rid of that notion fast, or your career will end right where it began. "The Queen, my lord, is dead " will be the zenith of your life in the theatre, and it will be hard to convince your grandchildren, as you sit before the fireplace forty years later, that you had a great potential career in the theatre, but that somehow the world missed out on the chance of knowing you. The roads to Broadway are paved with the broken psyches of talented yet unemployed actors. You need talent to be an actor, but talent is nothing you can acquire. If you've got it, you'll learn so early on. If you're without it, try some other profession. But if you've got it, don't delude yourself that talent will get you a career. All your competitors have talent too. You'd better have more in your theatrical trunk than talent if you hope to work.

TRAINING   There are 22,000 members in Actors' Equity Association, 34,000 in AFTRA, 38,000 in the Screen Actors Guild at present, and all of those actors have some form of training. It may be merely experience gained working in summer stock, or it may be formal training at some university or acting school which offers an intensive, three-year course in acting skills. And each year hundreds more arrive in Hollywood, New York, Sydney, and Toronto with some degree of training. Some will not even know why upstage is where it is and others will hold advanced academic degrees, like the MFA so popular today in American universities. But each will believe he is trained. How trained are you? Aren't your chances of employment likely to be improved in relation to the extent of your training?

It is true that your appropriateness for a particular role is likely to be more influential than your training in securing any single job, but it must be equally true that the more things you can do, the better are your chances for being appropriate. I recall auditioning a young actress in Hollywood for a role in a play based on Chekhov's novella *Late Blooming Flowers*. The interview went approximately like this:

> Me: Have you played any of the Chekhovian ladies?
> Her: How do you mean?
> Me: Well, have you seen any of the Chekhovian canon?
> Her: Well . . . I'm not sure . . .
> Me: What's your favorite play of Chekhov's?
> Her: I'm sorry, I don't follow your vocabulary.
> Me: I see . . . well, please leave your photo and resumé and I'll see if there's anything for you.

I have no idea if that young lady could act. Or if she could act any of the roles I was casting. But I knew I wouldn't have the time in rehearsals to teach her all she needed to know about Chekhov. Her lack of education lost her the chance to demonstrate her abilities. Her training for the theatre was inadequate.

This is not the place to engage in a lengthy discussion of variant forms of acting training or the values of education to an actor. Suffice it to say that no actor has ever had sufficient training or education, and that both are life-long pursuits for the serious actor. I was astounded and delighted to spend an evening once with Janet Suzman and Alan Howard of the Royal Shakespeare Company and to learn that they took it as a matter of course that they should read scholarly criticism about a role they were preparing. I was equally delighted to learn that Laurence Olivier, whose vocal instrument is regarded by many as exceptional, engaged a voice teacher for several months prior to beginning rehearsals to play the role of Othello. Training for the theatre is an unending activity, and its rewards are twofold: an ever-widening appropriateness for roles and the ability to perform roles richly.

What should you do about training? Get more. If you're getting roles in Hollywood and New York, consider classes that will expand your skills: singing, mime, fencing, dancing. If you're having trouble getting cast, consider going to some institution which will give you a firm basic approach to your work. If you're just starting out, select the finest and most exhaustive program your funds and time will permit you to follow. It is just common sense. The marketplace is jammed with talented actors. Increase your odds of employment by becoming trained as well as talented.

Unhappily, skills alone may not get you work. There is the tale of the young actor who arrived in Hollywood and struggled unsuccessfully for four months to get an appointment with an agent. Finally, through some contacts, he got one and arrived fifteen minutes before his four o'clock appointment. He had his photos and resumés neatly in his briefcase and he had just invested his last $15 in getting his hair styled. He was optimistic. He was ready to show his stuff. Four o'clock came and went. The actor reminded the battleweary secretary that he was to see the agent at four. "In a minute," she replied. Four fifteen. Four thirty. "My god, he'll be leaving shortly," thought the young actor, "and I'll have blown my chance." He approached the secretary. "Would you please remind him I'm here?" He returned to his waiting chair and she buzzed the inner office. Four forty-five. Finally the agent opened the door. "Come on in, I've only got a minute." The young actor scrambled into the office, trying gamely to retain his cool, and took a seat opposite the agent. "OK," said the agent from behind a frown. But the phone rang. And then the other phone. And the agent was on both. "No, Charlie, not without an out-clause after the first thirteen episodes . . ." "Hello Grace, listen, tell me the scenario. Well, read it to me now . . ." A phone on each ear, he looked up. "Go ahead, kid, show me what you do." The young actor stood, slipped off his jacket, walked to the window of the 17th floor office, opened it, and dove out. He swooped into the air, pirouetted in the air, did turns and flips out there in space, and then, in a final dazzling display, somersaulted back into the office and into his seat. The agent looked at him, eyes wide. He grabbed up his pencil and the actor's resumé and scribbled on it. "Right," he said, "I'll call you when we need someone for bird imitations."

No, in show business, skills are not enough. You also can use a bit of luck.

LUCK   If you are sitting in your apartment waiting for someone you don't know in Hollywood to discover you, just because of all those terrific notices in the local newspaper for your performance as the psychopathic young murderer in *Night Must Fall*, you are not likely to be selected to star in the upcoming episode of *Emergency*. Even though you are exactly right for the role, and even though you are exceptionally well trained. To be lucky in the theatre, you've got to be where the luck is and where you can help to make it happen.

Let me not deny that there is luck in the maddening world of the theatre. Consider Larry Sturhahn's interview in *Filmmaker's Newsletter* with Milos Forman, director of *One Flew Over The Cuckoo's Nest:*

> LS: The part of Chief Bromden was also perfectly cast. But I gather he was an unknown, and not an actor either.
>
> MF: In his case we were very lucky to find a big man who was an Indian and a good actor, although he was actually a rodeo rider. We had asked some connections in New Mexico and Utah to look for a 6 foot 5 Indian for us, but the results were zero. Then one day Mel Lambert, who knows all the Northwest Indians and even speaks some Indian languages, told us he had seen the biggest son of a bitch we ever saw!
>
> Jack Nicholson was flying up with me to see the hospital and meet the superintendent so we went to some kind of cocktail lounge to meet this guy. Suddenly the door opened and this *huge* man

came in! I really got excited, but there was still a
question as to whether or not this guy could do it.
The first thing I learned was that he was very
intelligent, which was encouraging because that's
a big help in acting. Then I did a short reading
with him and found him very responsive.

A star is born! If you are a 6 foot 5 inch Indian, can wait around
for another role like Chief Bromden, and can assume that someone will find you hiding in a rodeo, you have nothing to worry
about. Few actors are that patient. Most have to go where the
luck is, advance themselves, promote themselves, and then hope.
If you were lucky enough to have been traveling through Kuala
Lumpur, Malaysia, recently, you might have responded to this
advertisement:

Singapore Film Development (Pte) Ltd.

recruiting actors and actresses.

Applicants must be above 18 years old and under 30 with at least Secondary School education.
Successful candidates will undergo training for a short period before becoming film stars.
Please apply personally with 2 passport-size photos, your Identity Card and personal particulars at
ORCHARD THEATRE, Grange Road, on 26th, July, 1979 (Thursday) between 8 a.m. to 11 a.m.

You might well wonder at the quality of films made with actors
who have had "training for a short period before becoming film
stars."

In several places in this book, I'll be remarking on ways to help
shape your luck and places to be so luck can find you. Here,
merely accept that for those tens of thousands of talented people,
and those thousands of trained and talented actors, there will be
hundreds of lucky ones. Be one of those. Don't wait for your luck
to come to you; put yourself in its path. Become one of those
hundreds that the unemployed call "lucky."

CONTACTS   "It's not what you know, it's who you know" is
probably truer in the acting profession than in any other. Most
actors will tell you that 80% of their jobs come through friends.
Who do *you* know? To begin with, you know lots of people.
Every actor you know, knew, or will meet is a contact. Everyone
connected with any side of the entertainment industries is a

contact. There's no telling when you'll meet that person who will give you that piece of information which will bring you to the audition that will bring you work. Let's approach this a bit more systematically. Every class, every job, every party is a beginning place for contacts. Your teacher is a contact, because someone somewhere went to school with him and is now a director looking for an actor just like you. Every student you study with and every actor you work with is someday likely to be able to do you some good. Everyone you meet at a party, who works in the business may sometime or other know someone who's looking for an actor just like you. The number of your contacts grows in geometric proportion the longer you are in the business and the more you do.

Remember, however, that there are good contacts and bad ones. One guy who will badmouth you can do you more damage than you'd ever believe. Think of the conversation at the beginning of this prologue. I was only a visitor in that office, but I promise you I would avoid hiring that actor should the occasion arise. There are so many actors to choose from that no producer or director will knowingly engage a troublemaker or a nuisance. An actor who develops a reputation as a troublemaker has two choices: be so brilliant that everyone will tolerate you in spite of yourself (and I'll bet there aren't ten actors in America in this category) or get out of the business. Remember that while a director is hoping you are exactly what he's looking for when you meet him, another part of him is also asking that hard-nosed question, "Why should I hire you?" If he can find a reason he shouldn't, if your contacts have been negative, then you're in trouble. What is the moral of this? Well, nobody expects you to be Goody Twoshoes but the more people who like you, the more useful contacts you have. Remember, getting a job in the theatre is a bit like looking for the proverbial needle in a field of hay stacks. Any contact who can help you find the right stack has done you a lot of good.

Some actors are comprehensive and aggressive in their use of contacts. They keep a notebook of everyone they might consider a contact. Some divide the names in the notebook by function (director, actor, manager) and some by medium (stage, TV, film, regional theatres, summer stock). Some don't subdivide, but function on the "blanket" theory—the more people you're in contact with, the more your contacts can help you. At present my schedule permits me to direct a professional show only about once a year, and I am rarely in a position to cast more than the occasional small role. Even so, I receive at least 250 letters or postcards seasonally from actors who've worked with me or met me and who want to keep their names before me. For them, I am a contact. (Which just shows you what a desperate profession you have chosen to follow!)

Each actor must deal with contacts in his own way. And each must wrestle with his own integrity. All actors will say, at some moment or another, "I want to make it on my own." No one does! Get that naive thought out of your head as quickly as you can. Everyone takes assistance when it comes along, even if it takes the form of the agent's secretary telling her boss that you're a polite young lady and he ought to consider you. The degree to which you exploit your contacts is the only issue at hand, and you will have to work out that degree for yourself. Try putting the question in reverse. How much would you help a friend? Can you expect your friends to help you as much? Less? More? Your friends are your first contacts. And you are theirs.

EMPLOYABILITY   I probably should put this term in quotations to encompass a large number of traits that the actor must have if he is to find work. Each of these, in turn, is a partial answer to the pervading question in the mind of an employer, "*Why should I hire you?*" (If you can imagine that question asked by Jack Elam in the role of a Hollywood casting agent, you'll probably find the correct inflection for it.) The logistical truth is, nobody needs you.

"Why should I hire you?" I asked a student of mine. "Well, I'm cute," he replied nervously and self-consciously. "That might be a fair answer while you're still here in a school where we all care about you," I replied, "but you're not. And I won't." And that was the truth. I had just returned from directing a show in the League of Resident Theatres (L.O.R.T.) circuit and I hadn't given that young actor a moment's serious consideration during casting. There were many reasons for that, but the first reason, the first aspect of "Employability," is that he had a poor self-image.

As an actor you've got to know who you are. A young actor once auditioned for me with one of Coriolanus's speeches. I asked him why he chose it. Was it something he'd played? Had a teacher suggested it? Was he working on it in a class? "No," he replied, "I just liked it." I disregarded him immediately. He was 6 foot 1 inch tall and weighed about 150 pounds; he was a sunken chested, nasal voiced, midwestern country boy and could no more play Coriolanus than could John Wayne. The actor had an inaccurate self-image. That's a common problem for young actors just out of schools or training programs where they have been cast in roles they are wrong for, either because they were the best available in an impoverished talent pool or for therapeutic, "educational" reasons. The realities of the marketplace are hard ones for many young actors to accept. "Is there anything in it for me?" is one of the most commonly asked questions in the acting world. It means, simply, are there any roles in the show about to be cast for which I am the right type? If there aren't, let me not waste my time and psychic energy on the audition and let me not waste the director's time as well. An accurate self-image is essential to the actor. I will be forever thankful to that wise actor who came to me during a general Equity call and said, "Let's not waste each other's time. Either you want someone 6 foot 7 or you don't."

Your self-image has to do with more than your physical type, of course. If you are a clown, please don't audition for Hamlet. If you are a gorgeous ingenue, accept the reality that every straight director will want to fantasize about you and don't try to convince him you can also play the wicked stepsister. If you are a highly intelligent actor and have trouble playing stupid roles, know it. If you are a particular ethnic type, don't imagine you can play the W.A.S.P. boy-next-door.

Your self-image has something to do with how good you know you are. Now don't confuse the image of how good you believe you will become with how good you have proven you are. But if you've been terrific at school or in summer stock, there's evidence, in a certain arena, of how good you are. That evidence does not necessarily mean you are ready to play a lead on Broadway, but it does mean that you can be confident of your work in a more modest arena. When asked (even implicitly), "Why should I hire you?", you ought to be able to reply, "Because I have demonstrated that I am an effective actor, because for the money you're prepared to pay you'll not get better, and because I am _right_ for the role." If you can say those things honestly, then you've probably got an accurate self-image.

How do you know if you're _right?_ It's hard for actors to know how others perceive them. Here's a device which might help you learn how a director might see you when you come into an audition. Agree with three of your friends to watch a sequence of television shows over the course of a few days. Select a variety of shows: a soap, a sitcom, a western, a cops-and-robbers, a movie-of-the-week. Agree to watch the same programs—but each of you see the shows independently. For each of the shows (and for each of the commercials) write down the roles any of your three friends might play. Then, after you have completed these lists, get together to compare notes. Each of you will find out how the others saw you. If there is consensus among the three about particular roles, you will have a starting point for recognizing the kinds of roles a director might imagine you playing, the kinds of roles for which you are _right._

Not all casting is type-casting, of course. There are exceptions to all rules and the rule of type-casting is broken whenever a performer shows a director that the unique quality he can bring to the role is more valuable than his conformity to the director's preconceived notions of type. Marlon Brando's performance in _The Godfather_ is a fine example of an actor's proving a range and flexibility that no director would have imagined. If you are a flexible character actor, your chances of influencing a director's casting by an exceptional and particular audition are very real. At the same time, you are well advised to know how others see you, to know what type you will most typically be cast in.

Given a choice, I'll always work with someone I like. That's a second trait an actor needs to be "Employable"—a pleasing personality. Rehearsing a play is a difficult enough task without the added problems that abrasive personalities might add. Nobody is asking you to be a continual Pollyanna. Just be yourself—unless yourself is an abrasive, feisty, unpleasant self—in which case _be quiet!_ If you have learned through the years that the world does not find you to be an engaging and delightful social lion, then protect your "Employability" by being unobtrusive. Don't be a complainer ("The rehearsal room is too hot," "He held us two minutes overtime," "I was called today and he never even got to me"). Don't be a whiner ("Will we get a lunch break soon?" "I'm too tired to do that scene again today"). Don't be overly helpful ("Gee, I'd be happy to run lines with anybody who's having trouble"). Just be an efficient, cooperative professional. If you do that, you might find you're developing a pleasant personality, and when the director thinks, "Why should I hire you?", he may well answer himself, "Because you'll be pleasant to have around my life for the next four weeks." You will be developing that second trait the actor needs to be "Employable."

"Show me what you can do," the casting director says and leans back with his forty-seventh cigarette of the day. Well, what *can* you do? Can you sing? Hoof? Play the zither? Can you stand on your head and drink water while your ventriloquist's dummy juggles and sings Verdi's *Otello* with a Russian accent? The more things you can do, the more skills you have, the greater is your chance of being appropriate for the role being cast and the greater will be your "Employability." The continual expansion of your skills is a portion of your career, of your life. I engaged an actress recently who is a bona fide member of the Actor's Studio, an experienced and mature performer who has a responsible career on stage and in films and television. One day, over dinner, she confessed she had never been in a verse play, had never done any Shakespeare but hoped one day she could "get into Shakespeare." I was appalled. What did she do in her classes? Her continuing scene work at the Studio? Didn't she realize how she limited herself by her lack of skill with verse drama? Too many actors are like her. Too many actors wait until they have a role which will require them to learn a dialect or a skill. But when you've got the role, you don't have sufficient time to learn to fence—you must know how before you are cast so you can use the time available for choreography to learn a specific fight sequence. And if you know the dialect at the audition, you'll greatly improve your chances of being hired.

The final aspect of "Employability" is what I must call *good work habits*. And that's what the rest of this book is all about. How an actor manages his time, relates to his co-workers, comports himself with his employers and audiences alike. How he goes about doing his work.

The Importance of Behavior

It is not enough to be talented, not enough to be trained as a craftsman. It is not enough to be lucky and not enough to have wonderful contacts. A professional actor needs also to know how to behave as a professional actor ought to behave, but as too few do! This book is an attempt to provide actors with guidelines to professional behavior.

The two greatest enemies to good acting are time and a lack of self-respect. There is simply never sufficient time for the actor to do his work correctly. Time is money in the commercial world of theatre and the actor needs to invest his time constructively, efficiently, and intensely. Proper work habits will assist you to use your time well. When you behave properly, you will work effectively. You will discover that during the hours you will be given to rehearse a role, you are able to maintain your focus on the real problems at hand. Too many actors are destructively insecure and have so little respect for themselves and their craft that they waste their time and belittle their work by deluding themselves that divine inspiration will intervene and all will be well. They have little craft and therefore few ways to assist themselves, and so they waste their time and their energies on leaping irrelevant, self-imposed hurdles. Like: "I can't work on this scene until I have the right props." Or: "I need an audience to make me come alive." But the actor who has sound working habits knows what he can do in each rehearsal and between rehearsals. He knows how to help himself and the entire production. He knows how to respect his work, and that helps him to respect himself. That in turn helps him to use his time wisely, to behave as a professional.

A young, blonde, and attractive acting student at Temple University listened one day as her teacher discussed the importance of the actor's off-stage behavior. He was describing how a particular director and particular company tended to engage actors with compatible personalities. "My God," she exclaimed, "you mean if I want to act I've got to go to charm school?" The teacher didn't reply. He just nodded. But I could hear him think quite loudly, "Yes, you need to learn *how an actor behaves.*"

AUDITIONS

The Second Most Important Performance

Your audition is the second most important performance you will give in any role. The opening night performance, or the one that gets reviewed, is the most important. If you act well then, you will help your career in many ways. You will contribute to the possibility of the show's having a long and successful run and that means you'll be employed for a long time and the steady income you'll receive will be a welcome rarity in your life as an actor. Even if the show does not succeed, or has a fixed run, you'll have come to the critics' attention and whenever you receive good reviews you may be optimistic about other managements' interest in engaging you for future shows. But short of that opening night performance, the audition's the thing with which to catch the conscience of the director. If you give a poor performance at the audition, you'll never have an opportunity to give another.

Despite this obvious truism most actors audition poorly. I've heard it argued that actors do that as a way of providing themselves with an explanation for the rejection they know is the norm in the theatre. When they are not selected, they can always tell themselves they would have been had they known the play better, had more time to prepare, worn different clothes, done a more low-key audition, done a more flamboyant audition, etc. Whether or not this is an accurate interpretation of the typical actor's defense-mechanism-in-action, it is an observable fact that some actors come to auditions ill-prepared and that they then present themselves foolishly. As a very young actor I arrived for auditions at the Oregon Shakespearean Festival with expurgated editions of the season's plays. I was naive enough to have taken them from my mother's library, never imagining that some texts of the plays were incomplete. When I got the opportunity to audition, I was unable to follow the scene being read, was unable to say my lines (many of which were not in my text), and created a dreadful impression on the directors, I am certain. I would like to believe that was a major contributor to the poor casting I received that summer, though I must not rule out the possibility that other areas of my acting skills were equally deficient and that I received the casting I merited. (As I recall, my major role for that five-play season was the aged Host in *Two Gentlemen of Verona.*) There may be an occasional excuse for a lack of preparedness in the commercial marketplace where frequently it is impossible for the auditioning actor to learn anything about the play (or film or commercial) he is about to audition for. But I see this same failing among the actors in resident companies, where the season has been announced for months, and among students at schools where the actual scripts are available weeks prior to the audition period. I cannot pretend to assess the psychology behind such self-defeating work habits. I can only urge all actors to get them out of their systems.

Do yourself a favor. Approach the audition as a businessman would an interview. Do you think someone hoping to be engaged as an executive challenges his interviewers to discover his secret abilities behind the mask of seeming indifference and ignorance he presents? Not likely. He does everything he assumes to be correct protocol and good taste to advance himself, proclaim his abilities, and persuade the employers that he is the only person for the job. An actor ought to do the same. The protocol may differ, but the activity is essentially the same. Your task is to convince the director to select you and there are many things you can do to help yourself.

Types of Auditions

Auditions vary greatly in type and format and they occur in a variety of places. You will be well off if you've prepared yourself for these differing experiences. If you have not had a *real* experience of the varying types and places, you can help yourself and your friends by auditioning each other in hypothetical circumstances. Indeed, by playing the game of "Auditioning," you will have a chance to sit on the listener's side of the table where you will gain valuable insights into what the auditioner sees, hears, and thinks.

I have been auditioned in large, dark theatres, in offices, hotel rooms, automobiles, in a rented hall with a videotape camera rolling, and once at the beach. Offices and rented audition halls (sometimes used as rehearsal rooms) are the most common places for auditions, but an actor needs to be prepared for any emergency. What you can do in a theatre will not necessarily work for you at the beach. The low-key reading you do in an office will differ from the open-voiced presentation you might attempt in a rehearsal room. When you are preparing material that you might use many times, in varying circumstances, you'll be well advised to rehearse it in as great a variety of locations as you can arrange. Bore your friends! Do your selections in their living rooms, their offices, in classrooms, hotel rooms, corridors, parks— wherever you can and as often as you can. Don't make the mistake of assuming your inspiration will carry you through the audition. Would you venture an opening night unrehearsed? Why audition unrehearsed?

The most common form of audition is the interview. It is a portion of all auditions and is frequently the entirety of an audition, your only chance to present yourself. That is particularly true in Hollywood where virtually all small roles, particularly those beginners might hope for, are cast on the basis of appearance and personality. Interviews are equally common in New York, as an initial screening stage. Managements are required by Actors' Equity to hold a two-day open call for all shows and typically several hundred actors a day will be shuttled through a small room before a not very interested representative of the director. What does the auditioner look for in an interview? Physical type, vocal type, appropriate skills, and personality. Ninety percent of auditioning actors will be ruled out at this stage of audition. If the role requires a soprano to hit a high C and you flat the note, or have only six months of study listed on your resumé, you're out. At this stage the management is trying to select a small number of plausible actors: skilled, appropriate, pleasant.

A typical interview is conducted in the following manner. You arrive in a waiting room, corridor, or lobby and are given a number and usually an approximate time that number will be called: say, 4:10 P.M. (If the number/time is for much later in the day than the present time, you're frequently free to leave and return. Be careful to be back very early, however, as on rare occasions the casting line moves faster than anticipated and if you miss your turn you're out.) You will probably be asked to sign a list which is kept by the Assistant Stage Manager (A.S.M.) or secretary who is coordinating the day's call. You may also be asked to fill out an audition form which typically has on it blanks for your name, phone number(s), union affiliations, agent's name and number. You may be required to present your union card to the management or some representative of the appropriate union who is there to deny entrance to non-union actors. You may be asked for your photo/resumé at this point, or you may present it only at the time you are shown into the audition. Now ... you wait your turn! When it comes you will be ushered into the auditioning room and you may very well be introduced by name to the director or to whomever is present. There may be several people in the room: Production Stage Manager, Casting Director, Director, Playwright, Art Director, Producer, Sponsor, etc. Most will be seated behind a table and, typically, you will be asked to sit at a seat across the table. By this time, some thirty seconds into the interview, your fate is probably already decided. The impression you have made up to this point is very important. Now you will be interviewed. Typical questions posed to you will relate to your training, your recent work, your agent, your experience, and any particular skills you might have which are required for the job. Do you ride bareback? Can you speak German? Whom did you work with last? Next you will be thanked, told that you will be contacted should there be any interest in auditioning you further, and you will leave as you came in. The entire interview will not last three minutes in most cases.

The second type of audition is one in which you are asked to present prepared materials. Usually these are held by directors of permanent companies or summer stock companies looking for actors who will be engaged for all or part of a season and cast in a sequence of varying roles. This type of audition is conducted in precisely the same way as the interview except that you will be asked to present your prepared pieces. That may occur immediately upon your admission to the auditioning room, or it may follow a brief interview. I always interview actors first, so I know a bit about them, and so they have a chance to get some sense of the room they're about to work in. But many directors feel it is faster to see the prepared selection(s) first. Then, if they're not interested in the actor, they can save the time and labor of an interview. It is quite possible that you will be interrupted in the middle of your prepared pieces. There is no way you can know what interruption means. It might mean the director never wants to see you again in his entire life, or it might mean that you have shown what he needs to know for now and he will call you back later, or it might mean he's rushed and must move you along even though his mind's not made up at all. You will be tempted to interpret such an interruption as rejection. Don't. It may be, but you won't know that for a certainty. If you give up at this point you'll waste your chances in the remaining brief moments of the interview, moments in which something about you may excite the director sufficiently to call you back for a subsequent audition.

The third type of audition is one in which the actor is invited to read selections from the play(s) to be produced (or from some similar play which the director feels will give him a reasonable sense of the actor's abilities). Frequently this "cold reading" is done in conjunction with the audition in which the actor is permitted to present prepared materials, and almost always the readings from the script will be done following the presentation of the prepared selections. In most instances the actor will be asked to stand and provide ample space between himself and the director's table during a reading. Film directors are less concerned with that than stage directors, since the close-up is the important concern of the film director and he can see you better if you remain seated near him.

There are some directors who will coach you during auditions. Usually this happens only if the director has called you back, or if he is very interested in you. One director is renowned for stopping young actors in the middle of their prepared materials and saying, quite harshly, "No, no. Stop acting. Just say the words to me simply. Don't give me that bullshit. Start at the top." Many actors are so unnerved by this that they are too rattled to go on. But I've known actors that director has badgered, then hired, and given their first Equity jobs. Other directors will ask you to repeat all or portions of your selections, but with different actions or given circumstances pertaining. Allen Fletcher, then the artistic director of the Seattle Repertory Theatre, caused me to repeat Didi's speech from *Godot* ("Was I sleeping while the other suffered?") and instructed me to play this action: to share my happiness with everyone. Of course that made no sense in terms of the play. But it was his way of learning my flexibility, my ability to take direction, my control. (He didn't hire me.) On other occasions, directors may give you improvisations to do. This time-consuming activity is usually a sign that you are being given serious consideration for the role. Many film directors videotape all such improvisations as a way of learning what the actor's presence on film is actually like. Stage directors will frequently resort to improvisation as a way of learning the actor's emotional range. As Robert Lewis remarks in *Method—or Madness?,** casting must be done to insure that the actor can reach the role's most intense emotional moments. If you are asked to do an improv "cut loose."

Auditions are normally private affairs. Rare are the directors who will permit other actors to sit in the room while an audition is in progress. So don't bring your girlfriend along with the expectation that she can see how it all goes on. If you have an agent, and the audition is for a role that is important, and if the

*Robert Lewis, *Method—or Madness?* (New York: Samuel French, Inc., 1958).

director is really serious about casting you, your agent may accompany you. But that is unusual. No, the audition is a meeting between you and the director—one on one. And whether the audition is a limited one for a few actors who have been recommended by their agents or that actor's nightmare, the "Cattle Call," the rules remain pretty much the same. You will be given a number, a chance, and an exit. It is not a cheery experience, but remember, it is your second most important performance so you had better learn to cope with its possible rudeness, haste, and depersonalization. You must come to terms with the truth that you are one number in a Cattle Call and find ways to make the judges recognize that you are a prize steer.

Preparing for an Audition

At 3:30 tomorrow afternoon you have an audition. Maybe you've followed up a lead given you by a fellow actor, maybe you've learned of the audition from the Equity callboard, maybe your agent has made the appointment for you. No matter. You are the one who is going, whose employment rests in the balance. What do you do?

The first thing is to insure that all the things you need to take with you are in order. These are likely to include: photo/resumé, musical instrument, accompanist, your portfolio of pictures and reviews, special equipment, an appointment calendar, a notebook, medicines, and good luck tokens. The working actor needs to have these items ready at all times.

Your audition kit should contain several copies of your photo/resumé, your equivalent of the businessman's calling card. Just as there are many styles and formats for those little white cards, so there is an infinite number of ways that photos and resumés are prepared. Most young actors worry themselves sick seeking the "right" way to present themselves. They are wise to concern themselves about these items, but there is a truth to be told that may ease the neophyte's anxieties. There is no "right" way; there are only "wrong" ways. That is, no photo and no resumé is going to get you work—but many will lose you work. The truth here is a simple one. Each person who looks at the photo/resumé is human and subject to the inconsistencies that make us human. Each has his own prejudices and idiosyncracies and each will pass an entirely subjective judgment on the photo and resumé. What pleases one director will bore the next. You cannot win, if by winning you mean finding a 100% foolproof model. The important thing to do is to insure that your photo and resumé meet the most common standards presently in vogue.

Vogues in photo/resumés change with the seasons and the cities. What is true for New York this year may not be true for Hollywood. But the current fashion will become evident if you check several resumés or speak with an agent. You had best conform to the fashion, which means you must be prepared to spend a lot of money on photography and duplication at regular intervals in your career. If you have an agent, your problems are usually reduced. The agent will determine what is wanted from you. Expect, when you first get an agent, that all the photos you presently have will be discarded. The agent will require new ones, ones that conform to what he understands the fashion to be, and that conform to the way he wishes to market you. (Beware of the agent who accepts photos taken only by a photographer of his nomination.)

The present trend in New York is for 8x10, black and white, glossy prints of head and shoulders. Most are taken in natural light and are not "arty"—no extreme shadows, no profile lighting. The goal is to give a clear image of what you actually look like so that the director can remember you by looking at your photo. Good = it looks like you. Bad = it could be someone else. There is a prejudice against funny hats, eccentric wardrobe, or cutesy pictures. The trend in Hollywood the last time I worked there was for a 10x12 sheet printed on matte, grained paper with an 8x10 on the front, and a composite of smaller shots on the back, each in a variant pose and costume, and with the agent's name and number printed at the bottom of the sheet. These sheets were frequently three-hole punched to fit into a casting director's spring-binder notebook. Before you get photos made up, decide what market they're to be distributed to and then investigate the current fashions.

Resumés are not particularly common in Hollywood since what you look like is much more important than what you have done. Frequently an agent will not circulate your resumé unless it is a simple list of major TV shows you have been seen in recently, the film of which is available for casting directors to look at should they be interested in you.

In New York, the regional theatres, and the summer stock circuit, resumés are expected. Typically, these are typed on a piece of 8x10 paper and photo-duplicated so that one can be stapled (at all four corners, please) to the back of each photo—making a self-contained and easily filed credential. A resumé is like a piece of journalism; it must tell who, what, where, why, and when. At the top there should be salient information: your name, address, phone number, answering service phone number (unless you have a recording device on your home phone, as is presently common), your union affiliations, your age (or age range), height, weight, color of hair and eyes. Further down the page there should be selected evidence of your work: plays you've been in, the roles you played, where they were produced, when and by whom, and any notable information like the name of a prominent director or star who worked the production. Young actors frequently list items in this section which nobody cares about. Of course, at the beginning of your career you don't have a lot to list. But don't assume that quantity makes up for quality. Don't list *every* play you've been in since childhood. For example, I once played one of the cards in a production of *Alice in Wonderland* in which Richard Chamberlain played the Caterpillar, but that dubious credit has never appeared on my resumé. (I doubt if Chamberlain ever listed it either.) Resumés need to be revised each time you do a role that you believe will make the resumé look more impressive. Don't scribble the addition in smearable ballpoint. Retype and reduplicate and restaple. At the bottom of the 8x10 sheet you may find room to list any significant training you have had (or are presently taking) and any particular skills you have: dialects, athletic prowess, foreign languages. Since you are limited to one small sheet of paper and since you want it to appear neat you will have to be selective.

Some actors lie on their resumés. Directors suspect about 15% of the material on a young actor's resumé to be at least a distortion of the truth, at worst a bold-faced lie. If you don't include some kind of inflated material you may disadvantage yourself, since anyone looking at the resumé will assume there's an element of fiction about it anyway. What kinds of inflation can you use safely? Well, namedrop. If any director or producer or name player was in any way attached to the production, make certain that's noted in your resumé. If you were in the crowd for a one-week stock production of *Julius Caesar* with a featured star, you can say you played "with" the star. If questioned, you can hedge a bit and say that during discussions about a possible extension of the run you were asked if you'd be available to take over one of the supporting roles. Indicate the places you've worked by the name of the theatre, not the name of the college. Playing Casca at the Lobero Theatre in California is far more impressive than playing the same role for the University of California's Drama Department. Particularly, in that instance, because the Lobero is occasionally a home for professional shows, and a director might assume the show you did was a professional one. Overt lying cannot be recommended but inflation is as much a part of our theatre's economy as it is of our nation's. Happily, the more you work, the less you'll need to inflate your deeds. Time is on your side. You'll either develop a legitimate resumé or you'll be out of the business.

A large number of jobs you'll audition for require you to have some musical skills. Legit plays have songs in them, musicals are dependent on their scores, industrials are the same as musicals; even commercials frequently hire "singers." You must check that your needs for such an audition are in order. If you will be asked to play an instrument, you will be notified in advance. If you're going to play something (or accompany yourself as you sing), rehearse it exhaustively. The total effect of your presentation can be marred by inept musicianship. If your instrument is the tape recorder, bring along one that requires no time to set up—a transistor cassette machine is best. Make sure the batteries are new.

If you are doing a singing audition, bring your own accompanist. At many auditions an accompanist is provided and he is usually a surprisingly good and flexible pianist. But he hasn't rehearsed with you: he doesn't know the tempo, the phrasing, the shifts in volume and rhythm you will make. Singing with a pianist you've not rehearsed with is a bit like auditioning in a language you don't really know. Don't do yourself such a disservice. Even though it may cost you money (accompanists need to eat), bring your own. If scheduling is a problem, ask to have your audition time changed. Managements are usually happy to make an adjustment if it means you can have your own accompanist. They know the difference and they want to hear you at your best.

If it is impossible for you to bring your accompanist, at the very least bring your own sheet music—well marked with the dynamics that will help the pianist. Indeed, you should always carry sheet music for at least three songs with you: a ballad, a belt, and a folk song. Then, in the audition which wasn't going to be a singing one but during which the director suddenly thinks "My God, maybe I can cast her in the revue we're doing at the end of the season," you're ready. You can reach into your audition kit and "voila!"

There are three kinds of singers: those who can sing, those who can fake, and those who can't sing. Don't claim you can sing unless you really can—unless you have studied for a long time, can hit all the notes, and are in truth a singer of songs. It insults a director if an actor claims to be a singer and then demonstrates in the first six bars that he isn't. Directors don't like actors who fail to fool them. A faker of songs is someone who knows how to sell a song, can phrase exquisitely, hit enough notes to give the impression of melody, and charm the pants off you. Rex Harrison's performance as Henry Higgins is the standard example of a faker. A caution: a bathroom singer is not a faker. A bathroom singer is someone who is untrained—usually loud, uncontrolled, energetic, and unable to hear his errors—though usually in love with his voice. If you are a bathroom singer, you have two choices: study to become a singer or keep your mouth shut. An actor who does not sing is just that: one who tells the director he has not studied and is not a singer. Now, if the director says "sing anyway," go ahead. And be prepared to do so, with a well-rehearsed song that is simple, within your range, and presented without bravado. Let the director sell himself on the idea that he can make a singer of you. If you have flatly denied being able to sing, your integrity is fine. If the director then causes you to demonstrate that you can hit all the notes of the ditty to be sung and that your voice is a simple, unaffected, untrained one, he may be very happy. And when he's happy, you have a chance to work.

Some directors will want to look at your portfolio, so it is imperative you keep yours up to date and in your kit. A portfolio is merely a collection of additional photos and occasional reviews which might give the director a richer sense of you during an interview. Typically, the portfolio will contain a half-dozen 8x10s showing you in varying angles and poses: some full body shots, some mug shots. This is the chance for you to include your cutesy pictures and your cheesecake. You might also include one or two shots in extraordinary makeup and costume—as a way of reminding the director of your versatility. Any reviews you choose to include should be from the most prestigious productions you can offer. The rave you got from the college paper is of no use here. But the one line saying your performance was "strong" in a Shakespeare festival's production of *Timon of Athens* is worth including; that festival is someplace where critics are supposed to apply professional standards and where other fine actors may have worked before you.

Portfolios are not commonly looked at by directors of commercial shows in New York, but Hollywood casting directors like to see them because they can see how your face photographs from many angles and how differing clothes look on you. Portfolios are always expected if the call is essentially for modeling, whether you are in New York, Hollywood, or Baton Rouge. The three-hole binder is an acceptable style of portfolio, but in recent years portfolios have become increasingly elaborate. Many New York actors who seek a lot of commercial and/or modeling work carry a leather, zippered portfolio that is 11x14 or larger and that frequently has handles like a briefcase. As with photo/resumés, the fashions here are subject to change. Take a look at what others are using.

For many auditions you will need to bring along some special equipment: costumes or props. Make certain these are ready in your kit. If you're going up for a musical and you dance, make certain you bring along your dancing shoes. If one of your prepared selections requires a springblade knife with which you can safely stab yourself, bring it along—and check it first to insure that it is functioning correctly. I nearly cut off a finger once doing Jerry's final speeches from *Zoo Story*. The blood lent realism to the audition, but the director was more than a bit distracted by the accident.

Something needs to be said here about the medicines you should keep in your audition kit. Obviously aspirin, breath mints, cough drops, antacids, tissues, and bandages are essential. Additionally, some actors have been known to use tranquilizers for auditions; the most popular kind are, essentially, muscle relaxants, which do not affect one's mental capabilities. But I am strongly opposed to actors using any chemicals in their systems. If you are well trained, you should have a technique which will permit you to relax just prior to an audition, rehearsal, or performance.

A well-prepared actor will keep a small diary or calendar book, a small notebook, and a pen in his audition kit. The calendar book is used to keep all classes, rehearsals, appointments, auditions, and other professional dates recorded so you can avoid scheduling an audition at a time you're not free. The small notebook is for you to inscribe the names and phone numbers of anyone you meet (the director, casting agent, sponsor's representative) or the details of any information about casting you may learn in the waiting room.

Finally, there are your totems, your good luck pieces. Some are religious, some personal, some clichéd—it doesn't matter. If you get comfort from saying your rosary while holding your rabbit's foot, take those things with you. There's a vast amount of luck and whimsy in the casting process and if these items will help you relax and send out good "vibes," don't be without them.

Well, that's quite a list. Have them ready; auditions frequently come on short notice. My first New York job came like that. At 11:30 one morning a friend called and told me to hurry to the Playhouse Theatre on 48th Street. By 12:30 José Quintero had cast me in my first New York show. At 12:31 I was in rehearsal.

The audition kit should be a bit like a doctor's little black bag. It should have a small amount of everything you might need and it should be ready to go with you on any call. Some actors use briefcases to carry their things. Others prefer to appear more informal and use airline flight bags or army backpacks. All that really matters is that you have what you need when you need it.

☆ ☆ ☆ ☆ ☆

How much do you know about the audition you're going to? The second task before you is to learn as much as you can in order to present yourself as well as you can. I am depressed when I audition actors who could know something about the job they're seeking but don't. I suppose I'm least patient with students who saunter into an audition ill-prepared, mistaking their teacher for their friend, and not realizing the teacher has become director and that friendship has nothing to do with the casting of a play. These students (the most talented are frequently the greatest offenders) are teaching themselves very bad work habits. Their teachers are doing them a grievous injury by permitting such poor professional behavior. Sadly, the same poor habits frequently are found in the profession. I auditioned a company for roles in *Romeo and Juliet* recently and discovered that about 15% had never read it. When I was seeing actors for *Late Blooming Flowers,* that show adapted from Chekhov's novella, I knew the script was not available and so I knew no one could be fully prepared. But I thought some would have read the novella and that all would have some knowledge of Chekhov. I was wrong. One actor came in, described his background as "several films with Steve Reeves in Italy," and confided he'd never heard of Chekhov. I was dazzled by his arrogance, but I never gave him a thought when it came time to cast the production.

Where can you learn about the audition? Where did you first find out there was a call? If it was from one of the trade papers like *Variety, Backstage, Show Business,* or *The Hollywood Reporter,* there was certainly some information you could use as a starter: the name of the play or film, the ages and types of the actors being sought. If it's a published property buy it and read it. Next, inquire of anyone who might help you. If you have an agent, bug him until he gets you some hard intelligence. If there's a phone number with the announcement of the call, ring the people and seek whatever added information they will give you.

If the script is not otherwise available, try to get one from them. When you get to the audition, ask the other actors if they know anything you don't. Particularly, ask those who are leaving the audition: Did they do a cold-reading? Did they get any coaching inside? Ignorance is one of the actor's greatest enemies at auditions, one of the greatest contributors to anxiety. The more you know, the better off you are. Frequently the A.S.M. can give you information—a look at the storyboard, if it's a commercial; a look at the scene you'll be asked to read. That's another reason to get to the audition early.

When you have learned all you can, consider how to costume

yourself. Remember, this is a performance you're about to give, and your costuming is an important part of the effect you will make. If you know something about the play, try to wear clothes that will suggest the period or type of character you're hoping to be cast as. If *Virginia Woolf* is being cast and you're hoping to read for Honey, don't wear pants and don't wear anything with a plunging neckline. Wear an attractive and modest dress—as Honey might. Don't expect the director to be a superman who can see through the denim coveralls you're wearing to the fragile soul you believe you have underneath. When an actor walks in the door I want to see something like the character I'm looking for. Immediately.

As with all aspects of this profession, fashions change with the seasons and the geography. Actors in Hollywood need to present themselves differently from actors in New York. In Hollywood, what you show them is what they consider. If you (and your agent) believe you can get work as an unshaven, bead-wearing superannuated hippie, fine. Go to the call looking like that. And if there's a role for such a creature in the film, good luck. But don't assume you'll be considered for any other type of role. You may look at the script in the waiting room, discover you could play the juvenile's best friend, and ask to read that as well. You're wasting your time. You are seen as what you present. So be very careful how you choose to present yourself. In New York things are a bit more conservative. The East Coast businessman wears a necktie, and as an East Coast actor you must realize that the people putting up the money are expecting you to behave as a mature professional. They want you on time, sober, and working hard. If your clothing suggests you are irresponsible, you're not likely to impress them. In New York, and for stock and L.O.R.T. directors as well, you are seen as a talent which can be dressed to fit the role. The management wants evidence of two things at an audition: your skill as an actor and your maturity as a professional. They want to see you clean, well-groomed, conservatively dressed. In Hollywood you may get hired because you seem eccentric. In New York that will happen rarely.

Your kit's in order, you've studied the play you're up for, you've selected your costume. Now it's time to get *yourself* ready for the audition. Get a good night's sleep. Attend to your grooming carefully. Go over your prepared selections and songs several times. Pamper yourself at breakfast to help build your ego. Arrange your day so you're not rushed or frazzled. Walk into that audition at the peak of your powers. "Go out there and kill 'em."

How to Audition

Each audition is a five-part performance. Each is a unique experience, but each retains the same structure, and you will increase your chances of success in auditions if you know what to do in each part. Let us look at an audition as though it were the performance of a play.

First, you must arrive at the audition hall. Just as Equity requires you to be in the theatre thirty minutes before curtain time ("half-hour call"), so you ought to be waiting in the "wings" for your turn to audition well in advance of your appointed hour. You need time to learn what is to be learned from your fellow actors; to study the script of any scene you'll be asked to read; to warm up (if there's a place); to relax.

The second part of your audition performance is your entrance. As with any performance, you must have a precise sense of character, an action to play which causes you to enter, and activities you do (and lines you say) as a part of your first, entering beat. In an audition, as I mentioned earlier, the first thirty seconds can make or break you. So, decide who you are upon your entrance; get that characterization down pat. Are you the bead-wearing hippie? Are you the briefcase-bearing executive? Don't tell me you're yourself because that's nonsense. Acting is selecting those traits of the self to be presented in a given role. Well, what do you choose to present when you are ushered before the director? The role is yours to choose, but choose it with as complete a knowledge as you can acquire of the nature of the role you're up for, the type of theatre management that might engage you, the director's preferences. Keep your characterization close to your everyday manner, as you will have to repeat it many times, and if it is wildly improvised you may give a bad performance of it at a time you can ill afford to. One of the most spectacular entrances I've ever witnessed was a little old man who came to my auditions for an off-Broadway show, shuffled across the room schlepping his wrinkled topcoat, plopped his photo/resumé on my desk, and

mumbled a thick-accented "good morning." He then stepped back
and gave a knockout rendering of Hamlet's "O that this too, too
solid flesh." In clear diction, without accent. In excellent, youth-
ful carriage. With fine intensity, wit, and clarity. At the end he
schlumped, picked up his coat, muttered "dank you vary much,"
and walked slowly out. I was in love with him. I had nothing for
him in the show I was casting at that time, sadly, but he made a
lasting impression. I was delighted with his way of getting two
varied and entirely credible characterizations before me. I don't
know what he is like himself, but I know he can act. I can't
recommend such hijinks, but at that moment nothing seemed
more audacious, more theatrical.

Your entrance needs a clear action: to present yourself. That
will lead you to focus on yourself, rather than the coat or kit
you're carrying, to keep your energy centered in yourself rather
than bouncing about the room trying to discern which of the
people behind the desk merits your attention, to guide your
improvised dialogue towards the first person singular: *"I'm* glad
to be here. *I'm* Joe Doaks. *I* have my photo and resumé right
here." The auditioners already know who they are; they want to
learn about you. Present yourself. The beats of your first action in
the interview may be labeled thusly: to enter the room, to set
down what you are carrying, to introduce yourself, to take a seat.
If you do this, and if you have a clear sense of your characterization when you enter, you will make a concise, energized impression. There's no way of insuring you will be the person the auditioner is looking for, but you can be certain he has a sense of you
and won't discard you as being blurred, scattered, or vacuous.

The third part of your audition is the interview proper. At this
point the auditioner wants to learn several things. Have you the
appropriate physical and vocal qualities? Have you the requisite
training and skills? Have you sufficient experience? Have you
good professional working habits? Have you a personality he will
enjoy working with? The first of these is beyond your control. You
either are the body and sound he's looking for or you're not. Don't
fret about this. If the interview is protracted, there's a strong
chance you're appropriate. But if he cuts the meeting short, it
could also mean you're correct and that he'll call you back and
doesn't wish to take time now to do superficially what he intends
to do in greater depth later. Don't expend energy trying to

second-think the auditioner. Instead, accomplish *your* ends in the interview, play *your* action. He will question you about your skills and training, using your resumé as a point of reference. Here is a chance for you to elaborate. If you've studied stage combat with B.H. Barry, the brilliant and witty Englishman, slip that into your discussion. If you're a dialectician, demonstrate your skills in miniature. The auditioner will certainly question you about your recent work to assess your level of experience. Draw his attention to the most prestigious work you have done: theatres or directors or stars you've worked with. Don't assume the director has read your resumé; he's only just now scanned it. Point out those things you're proudest of. If you've been effective thus far, the director may be concluding that you have good, professional work habits. Support that notion by asking good questions. Find out when the production goes into rehearsal and what kind of run is scheduled. If you can make it appear you're doing a mental check on your availability at that time, so much the better. This is a good time to take out your calendar. That prop is a fine way of indicating you are an efficient and reliable workman. Ask if any of the key artists are already engaged: designer, costume designer, production stage manager. You may never have heard of any of them, but this will tell the director that you go about your affairs thoroughly. Lastly, inquire about the casting—when decisions will be made, whom you might expect to hear from, what telephone number you might call if you have questions that come up later. Again, if you can suggest you're awaiting word on another acting job, you will do yourself some good. *Never discuss money!* If someone raises the subject, and it is extremely unlikely anyone will, be charming and vague. "Well, let's not worry about that now," is usually enough to change the subject. You want them to want you and only then to negotiate a salary—when you have the upper hand.

Throughout all the beats of this brief interview, the director has been wondering if he would like to work with you—if he likes your personality. All you can do to guide him to the desired decision is to avoid seeming negative. Don't downgrade any work you've seen or any actors or directors who come into the discussion. Don't pass judgments on any plays or theatres. Don't badmouth anyone. The director does not care what your private opinions are and he definitely does not want to hire an actor who stirs up trouble or creates a negative working ambiance. Don't laud everyone either. The director doesn't want some dippy-tongued enthusiast about him. What he wants is a mature professional who may have firm opinions but who understands they are private and not for the public ear.

Throughout this third part of your audition performance your action has been to demonstrate your appropriateness for the job. The beats of that action: to elaborate on your skills, to reveal your sound professionalism, to make the director want to work with you. The more relaxed and unthreatened you seem in this segment of your audition, the better you will present yourself.

The fourth part of your audition performance will comprise the presentation of your prepared selections and/or a cold-reading. The auditioner's goal here is to learn how good an actor you are. Your action: to demonstrate how good an actor you are. You are working towards a common end, and you both want you to be excellent. Too frequently actors choke in this part of an audition because they mistakenly assume the director is out to get them. Your paranoia can be partially reduced if you can remember that he needs you to be right and that you are performing for a sympathetic audience.

A cold-reading means either that you've not seen the script before, or that you've had minimal time to look at it. There is always the exception. Apochryphal or not, a newspaper reported that Martin Sheen secured the manuscript of *The Subject Was Roses* twenty-four hours before his audition and memorized the entire role before he went in. He won the role and his performance established him as a working actor ever after. It is not necessary for you to be that fast a study. But there are many things you can do to aid yourself in a cold-reading. First, ask the director a battery of questions. What are the given circumstances of the scene? What is your character's major action? What are the relationships between your character and the others in the scene? Is there a particular quality the director wants to see? In addition to getting some of the information you need to play the scene sensibly, these questions will show the director that you have an efficient and precise way of working. He will increase his assessment of you as a professional.

When you actually begin to read, there are additional ways you can help yourself. Move far enough away from the director's table so that he can see you fully. Use a chair, if the scene permits one and if there's one available in the room (there almost always is). This will tell the director you know how to use space and objects in your work. Play your scene to the person you're reading with and not to the director. The interview is the time to talk *to* him. Now is the time to *act*. Unless the scene requires direct address to the audience, play to your partner. He will probably be the stage manager and he will probably read your cues intelligently and clearly, but probably won't "act" them. When I auditioned to replace as Tessman in Claire Bloom's *Hedda Gabler* the stage manager read Hedda—in red beard and glasses. No matter. My goal was, and yours should be, to play the action of the scene. If you can be sufficiently precise in your reading to make the stage manager "act," you will have acquitted yourself splendidly.

Always read more slowly than you would act. This is particularly true if you're auditioning for film work in which the actor's tempo is slower than the stage actor's; but it is also true for the stage actor. The director is not trying to learn if you can read intelligently. He wants to know if you can act—if you can play the actions of a scene, if you can fill out the subtext. If you read slowly you will permit yourself time to play the actions, or at the very least you will indicate that you understand the task at hand.

Lastly, when doing a cold-reading, commit yourself to an interpretation. Don't waffle, don't change in mid-scene, and don't generalize. Choose an action and play it. If it is the correct one, fine. If it is the wrong one, the director still will understand that you have the ability to play an action. He'll know it is his job to instruct you which action to play—and already he will imagine himself directing you. You'll be one giant step closer to employment.

The presentation of prepared materials is done in rather the same fashion as a cold-reading. Make certain there's ample room between you and the director's table. Announce the selections clearly. Too often the director misses the first part of your act because he's whispering to a colleague, trying to find out what selection you are doing. If you are doing more than one piece, announce both in advance, so that between pieces you needn't talk and the director can have a moment to think, make notes, or confer. If you've not yet had an interview or cold-reading, pronounce your name distinctly, spelling it if it is an unusual one.

Never narrate the plot of the play you are working from. I know one young actress who told the entire plot of *Our Town* to Morris Carnovsky. Can you imagine what went through that dignified gentleman's mind? If there is essential exposition, you may state it succinctly. "Gogo is asleep on the ground over here," I used to explain before launching into my audition speech from *Godot*. This prologue to your prepared selections is the place most young actors damage themselves. They become embarrassed at being themselves and mumble, shuffle, and generally fail to create the illusion of a self-confident professional. If you think the director will be patient while you "warm up," go ahead. Don't take more than half a minute, but if swinging your arms in the air and gibbering help you to relax, go ahead. Such a brief warm-up will also tell the director you have sincere and efficient work habits. Now, go ahead and do your scene as well as you can. At the conclusion, say "thank you" and return to your seat.

A great percentage of an actor's idle time is spent trying to select good audition pieces. Here are some guidelines to help you in your hunt. Have at least five selections ready to go at all times. Two should be classical in source, which means anything written before 1900, preferably in verse. One should be comic and one serious. The next two should be modern and realistic, which means anything written after 1920 and explicable in terms of contemporary psychology. The language of these two should be contemporary and prosaic. One should be funny and one serious. The fifth piece should be a wacky one—perhaps with a song in it, or it might be in gibberish. Whatever, it must be exceptional and distinctive, like the Lizard's speech from Albee's *Seascape,* or one of the Professor's lectures from *The Lesson.* All of the audition pieces should be selected because the characters are close to you in physical and vocal type and in age. Simply, they must all be roles you might play—that the director can believe you would play. I abandoned my pet audition speech from *Godot* the day I remembered the character is elderly; I am not. Your goal is to show what you can do now, not what you aspire one day to be able to play. If you know the role or roles the director is trying to cast, select something that parallels the role. When I was casting Hero in *Much Ado About Nothing* I was delighted to audition a young actress who did Juliet's "Gallop apace." In her Juliet I was able to discern my Hero. When I was casting for the twin role of Hugo/

Frederic in Christopher Fry's witty adaptation of Anouilh's *Ring Round the Moon*, I learned nothing from the young man who showed me Lenny's "mangle" speech from *The Homecoming*. Don't ever do something from the role you're seeking, unless the director instructs you to prepare it. The reason? Whatever you present will not be what the director imagines. Whatever interpretation you offer will conflict with the director's and he'll worry, "Oh dear, I'll have to kick all that out of him before we can begin to work," and he's already imagining the troubles he'll have directing you. You'll be one giant step further from employment. You'll frequently be asked to bring in selections which demonstrate your versatility and variety. Don't fall for that. What is wanted is a demonstration that you are a good actor. If presenting wildly varied selections is not your strong suit, don't play. Do what you do well. That's all. Inexperienced actors over interpret that request for variety and present their weaknesses instead of their strengths. George in *Our Town* and Nick in *Virginia Woolf* are both boy-next-door types, but the two present as much variety as is needed in a typical audition. If your variety is between a verse role like Proteus in *Two Gentlemen of Verona* and either George or Nick, you'll have satisfied the requirements of such demanding auditions as TCG's (Theatre Communications Group) or U/RTA's (University/Resident Theatre Association).

Don't do audition pieces that are done to death. I don't care how brilliant you are, if you're the twenty-second actor doing Edmund's "Now, gods, stand up for the bastards," you haven't got a chance. All that will be heard will be some amalgam of the hundreds of times the director has heard that speech; your audition will be obfuscated. Each year there develop fashionable pieces; try to avoid them. Last season directors were inundated with speeches from *Kennedy's Children* and songs from *A Chorus Line*. Young actors in their twenties find great intellectual identification with the monologues from *Kennedy's Children*. But the characters are all in their mid-thirties and the speeches make no emotional sense unless you are that old. The speeches are now so overdone they rival poor Edmund's invocation. The songs in *A Chorus Line* are marvelous, but each is based on the confession of a gypsy. Unless you've been one and unless you're close to the type the song celebrates, you'll seem phony—as well as superfluous. Pick pieces that are not overdone but are within your range, musically and emotionally. Don't try to bowl over the director with your power. Stay away from Lear's "Howl, howl, howl, howl." It takes about three hours of performance to get yourself to that peak and the same amount of time for us to get ready to hear it.

Where should you get your selections? From things you've played, pieces you've worked on in classes, things you've seen that you knew you were right for, plays you've read. Or adapt something. I am always delighted with audition pieces adapted from novels. Somehow I suspect the performer to be guilty of intelligence and that's exciting for me. A young actor once auditioned for me with a hilarious piece he'd written himself about a preacher in a men's room. I laughed hard and cast him quickly. No one can pick pieces for you, though people can and will recommend things for your consideration. The more pieces you develop, the surer you will be of having appropriate ones on hand for any occasion.

Your audition is nearly over. Your fifth and final part is your exit. A ham actor, when offered a role, will frequently inquire about his first entrance and final exit before accepting. Everyone wants to be clapped on the way off. In your audition performance clapping takes the form of the director's leaning over to the playwright and whispering, "I hope he's OK for you, 'cause that's the guy I want." The way you do your exit may have some bearing on the director's decision, so you ought to do it well—as a professional. Its beats are: to collect your things, to thank your auditioners, to go out the door. Your action: to depart. Do each of the beats briskly, but without rushing. Separate the three so that your "thank you" comes clearly and has precise focus. Your departure should be firm, assured, with no looking back and no diffusion of energy. As Bob Dylan says, "You're an artist; don't look back."

Do you believe all that happens within minutes? You've entered, talked, acted, sold, and exited again. Whew! Time to go have a beer. If you have done your performance well, you can do no more. If you have not, you might consider where you screwed up and take the time to prepare yourself for your next chance. Under no circumstances should you fret over your chances of success! Now's the time to forget the audition entirely. That may be hard to do, but you must teach yourself that discipline. If they want you, they know how to find you. If you spend the next few hours in intense worry, it will not be long before you find yourself in the intensive care ward with gastric ulcers. An audition is a little like a relationship. When it's over you've just got to walk away. There are some statistics which may help you accept that reality. A busy actor may have as many as two auditions a week, some thirty-five weeks a year. That's about seventy auditions a year. If you're good, and lucky, and "Employable," you may get engaged seven times: once for summer stock, once for a TV show, four times for commercial voice-overs, and once for a Broadway contract. Wow! That means that one out of every ten auditions has brought success. Would that were true! But for most beginning actors the percentages are much worse: one in twenty-five is probably closer to the figure. And there's no telling which of the twenty-five will be "it." So accept your lack of employment as a statistical reality rather than a personal rejection.

Nudity

The craze for nudity seems to be leaving the American theatre, I'm happy to report. Nudity is becoming accepted and is no longer a sufficient excitation of the audience to keep a bad play running. It still appears whenever there seems a sensible reason for it, or whenever a play can be excitingly theatricalized by it, but with the obvious exception of exploitation shows like the long-running *Let My People Come,* not many shows require actors to undress. Once the taboo was broken, once the newness of the phenomenon was over, audiences started looking at stage nudity with the same demands for credibility they make on other portions of a performance. Probably the silliest example of stage nudity I've witnessed was in the long-running West End hit *Abelard and Heloise* in which Keith Michel and Diana Rigg had a widely advertised nude scene. It went like this. Heloise comes up to Abelard's garret, they exchange a few lines, they embrace, her father enters and sees them, he has a heart attack, blackout. You don't have to be Neil Simon to know that's the stuff farce is made of—it's a broad, standard sketch from the days of burlesque. But in London's Wyndham's Theatre, nobody laughed. A hushed, nearly reverential tone prevailed, as the audience—well fortified against the supposed licentiousness with convictions of "artistic innovation"—watched as the renowned stars entered in a shadowy light from opposite sides of the stage, completely nude. They crossed to center facing one another, exchanged a few lines, lay down on the floor, and then looked up as Heloise's father entered, saw them, had his heart attack. Blackout. No one seemed disturbed by the truth that the actors' lack of clothing denied our imaginations the right to lascivious thought. No one seemed disturbed by the implausibility of what was seen. We were confronted, how shall I put it, with the limp reality that nothing was going on. A basically farce situation was made doubly farcical. I was wrong when I said no one laughed. I laughed. And was shushed for my lack of reverence as surely as if I had been in St. Paul's Cathedral.

How do you feel about appearing nude? You ought to come to terms with your feelings and thoughts about it because sometime or other the question is going to be put to you and a ready answer expected. It is possible you will exclude yourself from a role if you refuse to take off your clothes. If *Equus* or *The Architect and the Emperor of Assyria* is announced for the season of the company you hope to join, the question will arise. If the question is put to you in the general case, you can always reply, "I would want to see the script and discuss the scene with the director first." Any management will understand you to mean that if their intentions are not exploitative, you'll probably go along with it. If they show you the scene, you'd better be ready to make your answer.

In addition to having your mind made up about performing in the altogether, you have to be ready for nude auditions. If you're auditioning for a union job, specific rules exist. You can't be asked to strip until you've already been auditioned as an actor or dancer or singer. You can't be asked to strip unless an official from the union is present at the audition. (Do you wonder how the union selects people for that assignment?) But if the job is not under union governances, things are a bit uncertain. You can never be sure which mustachioed dandy in which hotel room is a legit employer and which is the proverbial dirty old man. The easiest way to handle the situation is to say, "Sure, I'll be happy to strip but my manager requires that he be present for any such call." If the auditioner is legit, he'll say fine and set up another call. If he's not, well, you're protected. Your manager, needless to say, is the largest, strongest guy you know. So if there's an unwanted advance you've got the marines behind you.

The Casting Couch

Casting couches are more common in movies about show business than in show business itself, but there is always the chance that some producer or director has seen too many movies and begun to believe the myth is real. Also, it must be confessed that the theatre is full of gorgeous people and that some employers are likely to try to take advantage of their positions of power to lure you to their couches. What to do? You can say yes, you can say no, and you can tease.

If you say yes, you are likely to get propositioned a great deal more often than you will be cast. Most theatre people take pride in their work and while some may dangle the carrot of a good role in front of you and try to get you to follow it right into the bedroom, they're not likely to give you an acting job by way of payment. You're better off finding your jobs on the basis of your talent and skills.

If you say no, things are quite simple. If you've rejected one of those directors who will only cast people he's slept with, you've lost the job. But those are few, and you'll not be long in the business before you know who most of them are. Their reputations are frequently nationwide. If you've rejected a director who makes his casting choices on the basis of his professional rather than sexual preferences, you've lost nothing. He'll cast the role as he would have anyway and he'll find someone else to take to bed.

Some actors will try to tease casting from any director who propositions them. They'll accept the dinner engagement, hint of their willingness to go to bed, but actually avoid it. Many will be coy and tell the director, "Oh, I really want to, but I don't want you to be influenced when you cast this role, so let's wait—and afterwards, no matter how you cast, we'll have a wonderful time." This form of blackmail is about as subtle as a thunderstorm. The director who falls for it is as stupid as the actor who believes it works. Teases of this type seem to me a dubious waste of one's time and energy.

Whom you go to bed with and why is entirely your business.

The only thing this book can recommend is that you ask yourself if the sexual offer is truly related to the professional offer, and if it is, is it worth it?

Negotiating a Salary

It is hard to work with someone if you've been fighting about money. The trust needed for theatre people to work together is extreme, and if there have been anxieties during the negotiating phase, it is sometimes impossible to work fruitfully. So the first notion about salary negotiation is to avoid it.

That's the major function agents perform and it is a very valuable one. If there is to be haggling over salary, out-clauses, residuals, or any of the innumerable business details that are a part of the legal contract you must sign before you go to work, let the agent do it. That way, there are never bad feelings between those of you who must work together.

If you don't have an agent, what can you do? One course of action is to accept whatever is offered as the salary. You either take the job or you don't, but you don't haggle. Another is to use the manager ruse again. "You'll have to call my manager," always gives you time to think about the offer. (In this instance you can select your manager on the basis of diplomacy instead of muscle.) Your friend the manager can then engage in a sequence of phone calls with the employer through which he can request whatever you tell him to request. And later, once you report to work, you can feign ignorance of the entire negotiation. But sometimes you need to act on the spot. The job is offered, a salary is quoted, and you're uncertain. You want more, but don't want to damage your working relationship. The easiest way to negotiate is by introducing your salary on your previous job, which was always a bit higher than you hope to get on this one. Here's a typical negotiation:

> Them: We want you for the show. We're paying $265.
> You: Hmmn!
> Them: It's the same for everybody who's working the show.

> You: I don't know. Last job I got $315.
> Them: Well, we couldn't meet that.
> You: What could you do? I mean, I don't want to go backwards.
> Them: Well, I'll tell you what. If you don't tell any of the others, we'll go to $285.
> You: OK. That's fine. Thanks.

The truth of the job market for beginners is that you'll be so happy to be offered the job you'll take anything they say. But when you get a bit more established and feel you can command a slightly higher wage, this is a reasonable way to approach things. You'd better take their compromise offer and not haggle further or you'll defeat your purposes.

A caution about kickbacks. Let's hope you never run into this, but it exists, so be prepared. You get offered a job and the salary agreed on is $150 a week. But the producer looks at you, with a carefully rehearsed hang-dog look, and says he can't ask you to sign the contract just yet because they're having a little trouble raising the last part of the capitalization. He continues that if each of the actors would agree to deferring $100 a week during the four weeks of rehearsal and first week of the run, they'll be able to get the show open. And after it's a big success, you'll get all the money you're due. Watch out! I fell for that on the first Equity show I directed. Someone out there still owes me $750. Some producers are even bolder and more vicious. "Look, we tell everyone it's $150 a week, but if you want the job you gotta kick back half to me under the table." Sounds like a 1930's Warner Brothers movie? Well, it happens. What can you do? Measure how much you want to do the show. What you will get from it. If you're not infringing upon any union regulation or breaking any law, make whatever decision you feel is in the best interest of your career. But measure the real amount you'll receive as your salary, not the fictionalized amount written on your contract. If the experience and exposure are valuable to you, if you can afford to work for what is offered and still eat, and if you're not bothered by the morality of it, make your own decision.

REHEARSALS

Repetition

Watch a runner prepare for a track meet. The event he'll compete in may take less than ten seconds to run, but he will spend months training for it — rehearsing. Watch the kinds of things the athlete does. Here's a partial list:

> He conditions his body through a rigorous set of exercises which do not appear to have any immediate relationship to running: push-ups, sit-ups, etc.
>
> He runs great distances, developing his stamina; frequently he alternates between sprinting, jogging, and steady pacing.
>
> He practices each of the parts of his event: the start from the blocks, the early acceleration, the final spurt, the reaching for the tape, the cooling down.

49

He runs practice heats—over and over and over again.
He studies his work with his coach, using films as a
way to see the action objectively.
He studies the way others run, either through films or
in person.
He studies physiology, to learn how to control the
muscles which will help him run fastest.

Acting is like running. The sprint of performance requires
weeks of training. The best actor, like the best runner, is well
prepared for the event. His skills are honed sharply because he
has known how to prepare himself. He has used his time wisely,
has known what to do in each phase of his preparation, and has
focused his energies initially on the training process and only
finally on the performing process.

Most actors do not know how to rehearse. Their rehearsal time
is spent in repeating rough imitations of imagined performances.
They know what the final effect intends to be and they hope
through an unstructured process of continual refinement they
will arrive at it. All too often their method of work is to "try
harder." Very few actors have a method of working which permits
them to focus on specific tasks in a given rehearsal. As the runner
needs to work on his starts, the actor needs to work on creating
credible transitions from each emotional beat to the next. As the
runner needs to study films of his practice heats to analyze his
work, the actor needs to analyze his script to perform well.

Some actors only wish to perform because what they want
privately from their work are the rewards their egos receive from
public approval. Accordingly, they only perform; they use
rehearsal time as a mock performance, secretly casting the other
actors and the director in the role of audience. Such actors don't
understand the nature and purpose of the rehearsal period, and
their finished work is the weaker for it. A true craftsman enjoys
the process through which he achieves his ends. The potter enjoys
the feel of the clay as it turns through his hands. The runner
enjoys the feeling in his legs when his start from the blocks is
smooth. The actor enjoys the rush of emotions he recalls. A true
actor is one who enjoys performing and also enjoys the creative
period of rehearsals.

Rehearsal is an imprecise word. In *The Empty Space* Peter

Brook reminds us of the French term and gives a fine description of the activity:

> *Répétition* say the French, and their word conjures up
> the mechanical side of the process. Week after week,
> day after day, hour after hour, practice makes perfect.
> It is a drudge, a grind, a discipline; it is a dull action
> that leads to a good result. As every athlete knows,
> repetition eventually brings about change: harnessed to
> an aim, driven by a will, repetition is creative. There
> are cabaret singers who practice a new song again and
> again for a year or more before venturing to perform it
> in public: then they may repeat this song to audiences
> for a further fifty years. Laurence Olivier repeats lines
> of dialogue to himself again and again until he
> conditions his tongue muscles to a point of absolute
> obedience—and so gains total freedom. No clown, no
> acrobat, no dancer would question that repetition is the
> only way certain actions become possible, and anyone
> who refuses the challenge of repetition knows that
> certain regions of expression are automatically barred
> to him.*

Your acting will improve as your rehearsing improves. It is common sense. Actors who know how to rehearse will acomplish more than actors who don't. A production that has six weeks of rehearsal will be richer and more finished than another that has only one week to rehearse. The greater the *répétition* the greater the chances for quality. But time is money in the economic reality of the English-speaking theatre. Rarely will you have sufficient time to rehearse your work satisfactorily. Acting is too frequently a race against time, an attempt to accomplish work in one-half or one-third the required time. The actor who uses his rehearsal time efficiently will help himself and his fellows. The actor who understands how to aid himself and his fellows through professional work habits is one who knows how an actor behaves.

Basic Etiquette

"Good morning." "Excuse me." "Thank you." "You're welcome." "Have a nice evening." "Goodnight now." Another civil day done.

*Peter Brook, *The Empty Space* (New York: Avon Books, 1969).

Those catch phrases by which we tell others that we respect them, their time, and their space are essential courtesies for the intense world of rehearsals. Many actors intentionally omit these from their conversations as a way of telling the world that they are a special, neurotic, pampered, privileged class. They use rudeness to support their puerile self-images as society's outcasts: the too-sensitive "artists" who can't be bothered with mundane civilities. What garbage! All they are is rude and disruptive; the result is that they create an abrasive and divisive ambiance at rehearsals. Such behavior is selfish and counter-productive. If you greet someone with a pleasant and modest "Good morning," and he fails to respond, or grunts condescendingly, you are unlikely to open yourself to him in the intimate scene you must rehearse fifteen minutes later. The theatre is a cooperative art form in which everyone must find ways to co-exist and contribute. Civilities help to create a working circumstance in which openness, mutual respect, and cooperation are the norms. "Excuse me," "please," "thank you," and "you're welcome" must be as basic to the actor's vocabulary as "line," "cue," "prop," and "make me a star."

Along with verbal civility, promptness is of paramount importance—to your own work, to the collective work, and to the management that is paying you. Actors get confused about what they have been hired to do. They think it is to act well. That's wrong. Actors are hired to work as hard as they can for a specific amount of time: a certain number of hours a day for a specified number of six-day weeks. When the choice was made to hire you instead of the others who auditioned for the role, a decision was made that was based on qualitative grounds. You were believed to be the best actor for the role. Once that decision was made, qualitative considerations were put aside, and time considerations became of paramount concern. Your time is what has been purchased, and you have a legal obligation to deliver it. The management has every right to expect you to be in the rehearsal hall and ready to begin work precisely on the minute you've been called.

You owe it to your fellow actors to be prompt. If a play has a cast of twelve and you're five minutes late, the loss is sixty minutes of collective rehearsal time. Rehearsal time is a very precious commodity, and it is irresponsible to waste it. In addition to the real, measurable waste of collective time, tardiness will set everyone on edge and the subsequent rehearsal will be much less productive than it might otherwise have been.

You owe it to yourself to be on time. If you have been working soundly, if you have done your homework between rehearsals, you'll be anxious to get to the rehearsal early. You'll know you need every available minute to explore with the others the work you have done privately. Time is the enemy of theatre; you must make the full use of it.

The tardy actor is unwanted. I have fired a professional actor who could not get to rehearsals on time. I have replaced student actors for the same reason. Usually, when an actor is late, I have the stage manager inquire if he had phoned in to notify us in advance of the difficulty or if, upon arrival, he had given an acceptable reason for his delay. (Few reasons are acceptable!) If there has been no explanation I usually say something like: "You are five minutes late. That's cost us sixty minutes of collective work and untold aggravation. If you find you are going to be late again, simply do not bother to come to rehearsals at all. I shall have replaced you before you get here. That applies to everyone in the cast. Now, shall we take places for today's work, please? Thank you."

☆ ☆ ☆ ☆ ☆

An actor who has "Big B.O." is either a star whose name on the advertisements insures sales in the box office or an actor who smells badly. How do you smell? Would you like to embrace you? An actor's hygiene is an important component of his professional behavior.

When you come to rehearsals, you are coming to work. Your work necessitates that you mix with others, and your personal hygiene can have an important impact on the effectiveness of that work. To begin: bathe. The English-speaking world is fanatical about cleanliness, placing it next to Godliness in its homilies and before everything else in its advertisements. We are conditioned to support a multi-million dollar industry which is dedicated to removing from us every odor that is natural to us naked apes. We are taught to obliterate body odor, foot odor, underarm odor, breath odor, and denture odor. Now, you may disapprove of this aspect of our society, but as a professional actor you must accept that you are the "abstract and brief chronicle" of your times. In future years, when our theatre practices are studied for revelations about our social customs, scholars will look at all those commercials and say with confidence, "Late twentieth-century man did not stink." As our society goes, so goes our theatre. And so must you. I don't care what you believe in, if you smell badly I don't want to rehearse with you. If you've come to rehearsal directly from playing basketball, I don't want to embrace you. If you've had a splendid Italian dinner during rehearsal break, I don't want to kiss you. At best, bathe before—even if you're pressed for time, even if you've been going to school all day prior to rehearsal. At worst, spray yourself with something inoffensive and gobble down some breath mints. That's why you keep them in your rehearsal kit.

Next, after your body is purged of its anti-social odors, attend to your grooming. The clothes you wear to rehearsal will have an effect on you as well as on the actors you work with. You should always come to rehearsal in relatively clean and tidy clothes and you ought to select clothing that provides you with some semblance of the "feeling" of the character and period you're working in. This will assist you in your own work and it will make it easier for your fellow actors to relate to you. If you are playing Lady Sneerwell and you arrive in Levi's, boots, and halter-top, you are not likely to "feel" particularly Sneerwellish, and the gentlemen in the *School for Scandal* are going to find it difficult to imagine your character. If you are playing Biff Loman and you arrive in Danskins, you're going to seem silly trying to pull that length of rubber hose out of your pockets. And the incongruity of your gesture will impede the desired flow of the rehearsal.

In addition to your clothing, you must pay attention to your hair: that on your head and that on your face. Too many actors disadvantage themselves and their fellows by arriving at rehearsals with their hair unkempt: unwashed and covered with dandruff, or recently washed and still in curlers. How can Romeo say "it is the East and Juliet is the sun" when he's looking at a head covered with hardware? How can Juliet reply when she's looking at a two-day beard stubble? Since the mid-1960's, when men's fashions in hair grooming embraced all variants of facial and head hair, male actors have become self-indulgent and

counter-productive in their work by placing their private preferences above their professional needs. I've encountered actors
cast in plays set in the 1920's, when the fashion in men's hair was
quite short and close to the head, who have resisted haircuts and
insisted on wearing ponytails. They were not cast as ponies, I
frequently remarked, and offered them the choice of a haircut or
dismissal. I worked with one particularly foolish young actor who
resisted shaving his beard, although he was playing a sergeant
on an urban police force, a role which could not permit facial hair.
(We had checked the regulations of the police force in
Philadelphia and had learned that the length of sideburns and
mustaches was stipulated and that beards were prohibited.)
Every other day I asked the actor to shave, so his fellow actors
could begin to see his face, to see him as the sergeant. He resisted.
Finally, five days before we were to open, he shaved. I don't know
or care why he delayed; it was clear the actor was painfully un-
professional in his approach to his work.

☆ ☆ ☆ ☆ ☆

There are four R's to remember as basic etiquette: *Respect the
Space, Respect the Time, Respect the People, Respect Yourself.*

RESPECT THE SPACE   You will work best if you treat your
working space as just that—a place to work in. That means the
only things in it ought to be items related to the work. Here's a
list of items commonly found in rehearsal halls and theatre auditoriums that are destructive to good working conditions: partially
eaten sandwiches, paper cups, cigarette butts, tea bags, old books,
abandoned clothing, crumpled cigarette packs, dogs, babies,
friends, newpapers, umbrellas, correspondence, notebooks, used
chewing gum, unused chewing gum, stage mothers, photo
albums, telephone books, and diaper bags.

Think of your doctor's office. Do you remember seeing any of
the items on this list in his examination room? How about in the
conference room of a legal firm? How about a chemist's labora-
tory? Those professionals seem to keep their spaces reserved for
group work in sensible order. A place of work is not a clutterbox
nor a dumping ground for personal refuse. Historically, actors
have had the reputation for being slobs. Perhaps their slovenly

behavior has resulted from that same attitude which has made some of them rude.

Acting students are among the worst offenders. Perhaps they are at an age of social rebellion. They have only recently left home environments in which they misinterpreted mutually accepted social behavior as parental constriction and are now living in dormitories or apartments in which no one forces them to pick up after themselves. Perhaps they import that adolescent behavior into their working environment. Or perhaps they are spoiled by the availability in most schools of a labor force of undergraduate lackeys who will pick up after them. Whatever the reason, the work habit is a deplorable one and debilitating to the group's goals. (In schools, where the teacher-director has some authority, it is desirable to build a "policing the area" call into the end of each rehearsal. That will relieve the stage managers from unpleasant duties which are not necessarily their responsibility but which too frequently fall to them by default. It will also help the actors to learn mature professional behavior.)

An actor's working space extends beyond the rehearsal hall or stage itself. It includes the auditorium of the theatre, the wings, the lobby, the dressing rooms, the box office, the toilets, showers, makeup rooms, and indeed any part of the rehearsal or performance complex. Actors spend an immense portion of their waking hours in the rehearsal space and frequently mistake it for their living quarters. They forget that the space is owned by someone else and that they are guests in it and ought to behave accordingly. An actress at Temple University's Stage Three grew very angry when she discovered her makeup had been removed from in front of the mirror she used nightly. She had forgotten that the theatre was also used by a company performing children's theatre, by musicians preparing a concert, by the management of a cinematheque, and on occasion by the University's guest lecturers. She had forgotten she was not in her own home.

RESPECT THE TIME   Promptness is a postulate of mature professional behavior that applies throughout the rehearsal period. It means that a one-hour lunch break finds the actor returned, warmed-up, and ready to rehearse fifty-nine minutes after dismissal. It means that a ten minute coffee break is no longer than ten minutes. It means that the actor who just exited does not wander off immediately and does not waste the company's time looking for him, should the director choose to repeat the scene. It means that the actor who is not working on the set is precisely where he has told the stage manager he is, and can be summoned without undue delay.

Actors must respect the time of everyone working on a production. When it is their time to work, they have the right to expect the full concentration of the director, stage manager, and other actors. When it is not their time to work, they must not intrude on the working time of others. Sometimes it is difficult to know when it is the actor's time, but a bit of sensitivity melded to a bit of experience will help the beginner to an awareness of the rehearsal's progress that will reveal this to him. A common error is for an actor to complete his scene and to want—right then—to discuss it with the director. The director may wish to proceed into the next scene, saving the discussion for a later moment in the day's rehearsal. The actors who are on stage and working do not want their time interrupted. The exiting actor should assess the situation before blurting out, "Hey, was that what you wanted?"

RESPECT THE PEOPLE   A camel is a horse that has been designed by committee, the old saw has it, and a performance is an event shaped by a cooperating group of theatricians. If the shape is elegant, proportionate, and efficient, an audience will know the group has worked well and respected the mutual contributions of all members. If a performance is as lumpy as a camel, the audience will know it is in for a bumpy ride. A one-hump camel may occasionally succeed in the race for large weekly grosses, but a two-hump camel is usually scratched before the race begins. The actor can help the group avoid creating a deformed dromedary by respecting the efforts, intentions, and accomplishments of the people he works with.

Two general practices the actor ought to observe in dealing with his fellow workers are abstention from offering advice and aloofness from the rumor mill. For inexplicable psychological reasons, many actors like to express their opinions on all sorts of subjects. The nature of theatrical advertising, the structuring of the rehearsal period, the construction of sets, costumes, and props, the skills of the company photographer, the layout of the program, the length of intermissions, the prices of tickets, the literary style of press releases, the ushers' uniforms, the skills of the choreographer, musical director, and dialect advisor: these are a representative sampling. Most actors' comments on others' work is negative and it seems evident they are seeking to lay the blame for the show's possible failure on someone else's shoulders. Well, don't do it! If someone asks your opinion of his work, you have three ways to reply. You may be complimentary. You may confess you don't know anything about the work and refuse to comment. You may offer concrete advice *only* if you have done that type of work yourself professionally and are *certain* the advice you're giving is accurate and applicable. If the costume cutter asks what you think of the skirt she has just fitted on you, you may say "terrific." If the PR director asks your opinion of the design for the poster, you may say, "I don't know anything about how to sell a show—I hope this will." If the stage manager asks you the best way to give an actor a cue, and if you have stage managed and dealt with that problem, you may say, "When I did it I raised my hand for the warning and then pointed at the actor for the 'go' and it seemed to be a clear cue." If no one asks your opinion, don't offer it! You don't want a lot of people telling you how to feel credible terror in your big scene, and they don't want you telling them how to do their jobs. They are professionals, hired because they know their work. So are you. Respect each other.

In every show, in every company, in every theatre school, on every tour there is a rumor mill. Nobody ever knows how the rumors start, but everyone has seen how they fly, multiply, develop, and disrupt. The actor is usually one of the least informed people working on a production. Administrative decisions are made without his awareness and artistic decisions are made without his consultation. Accordingly, the actor is typically the last person to learn truths and facts. At the same time, the actor lives in an intense world that is all but hermetically sealed from the rest of the production's workers and within his tight little world he begins to believe the show is all about him. Is it not the actor who will be the life of the play once it opens? Is it not the actor who must go out there and face the audience? Is it not the actor who risks all? Well, not exactly. For example, the actor rarely risks any of the $450,000 it takes to get the show open. And, despite the possible embarrassment he may feel should the performance be poorly received, he does not risk the damage to his career that the playwright does. There is more than a modicum of truth to the cliché that good plays are well acted while bad ones are poorly directed. The actor's belief that the world revolves about him is probably what makes him an actor, but it is not what makes him a sensible member of a company—one who resists believing in, propitiating, and encouraging rumors.

Rumors tend to deal with either events or people. Either they suggest that the opening is postponed and the costume fitting cancelled or they suggest that the director is being replaced and the spear-carrier is sleeping with the ingenue. To believe rumors is naive, to start them is corruptive, and to support them is divisive. When you hear a rumor that troubles you, ask the most informed person you can of its accuracy. That will be the stage manager, if it deals with events, and the director if it deals with artistic decisions. If they are responsible professionals, they will tell you the truth if they know it and are permitted to publish it. They will tell you they don't know if they don't know or if they are constrained by their employers from discussing the matter. In either event, you must then function as though what you've been told is what you need to know—and go on about your work. I was in a show in California and heard a rumor that an actor was to be replaced—yet I saw him at the rehearsal. I approached the director at a break and discreetly asked about the situation. "I'm not free to discuss it," he said. I understood him to mean that it was probably true, but that he and I should continue as though it were not. The reason? The replacement actor was not available until the following day. There were several scenes remaining that day in which the character appeared. Everyone needed to function as though no change were imminent, so that efficient use could be made of the rehearsal time. If the actor who was to be dismissed knew he was about to be canned, the rehearsal would have been awkward and minimally productive. I helped all of us get on with our business by keeping my mouth shut.

RESPECT YOURSELF   Actors are a little bit in love with death. Think how many catch phrases suggest it. "I'm going to kill 'em tonight." "I'm dying out there tonight." "The show died last night." "Breathe some life into it, will ya?" "If I go out there like this they'll murder me." "It'd be suicide to play it that way."

There is something about the actor that is self-destructive, that flirts with death. There is something about the actor that welcomes failure and it takes a strong actor with a lot of self-respect to overcome the temptation to fail. Self-respect is gained by improving one's skills, by experience, by longevity, by meeting challenges. The challenges the actor meets during rehearsals are many and his work will be good in relation to the way he meets them, in relation to the degree of self-respect he has. Many of the challenges have to do with the art of acting and are not my concern here; others have to do with the habits of rehearsing and are.

The sprinter can't run until he's warmed up and the actor can't rehearse until he is warmed up. The warm-up exercises are different, but the relationship between preparation and execution is identical. The actor needs to warm up his body, to make it flexible, responsive to his needs, and quick to respond to stimulation. Most actors learn a set of warm-ups during their training and then abandon them ever after. They are telling death they can be seduced. Of course there are troubles with doing the kinds of physical exercises that most actors know. There's rarely an ideal place to do them and actors are usually afraid of the ridicule of their peers. Imagine going into a rented rehearsal hall and starting in on a series of physical exercises. Why, the other actors might look at you, smirk, and scoff. If that bothers you, do your exercises at home, before you come to rehearsals. Then you will need only a few brief, selected exercises to be ready to work. On the other hand, if you respect your work enough to bear their ridicule, you might shortly find others joining you. Your self-respect might be contagious.

The actor needs to warm up his voice, to loosen the muscles, clear the resonating chambers, re-tune the ear. These exercises may take five or thirty minutes, depending on the type of role you're doing. If you sing, you should warm up that carefully trained instrument for a long time. If you're doing a prosaic modern play that requires few stretches of your vocal instrument, you might get by with a few scales and tongue twisters. Again, if you're embarrassed to do this in a corner of the rehearsal hall, do it at home, in the car, or in the bathroom. But do it. Respect your work enough to prepare yourself for it.

The actor needs to warm up his senses of observation, concentration, and emotional recall. These exercises can be done privately and in almost any location. The director of the Emerald Hill Theatre Company in Melbourne used to begin each day's rehearsal with an observation exercise. All actors were responsible for having observed someone on their way to work in the morning. One actor was selected at random and required to enact that person. The on-going exercises in observation insured that the actors arrived to work ready to apply their observations of life to their work. Similarly, concentration and emotional recall exercises could be done while riding a subway or waiting for a bus. If the emotion to be recalled is one required for the role being rehearsed, think how ready the actor will be when "places" is called. Think how he will have met the challenge of rehearsal and how he will have built his self-confidence and increased his self-respect.

The actor must come to rehearsals in optimal physical condition. That means he needs to have had sufficient sleep and a sound breakfast (or supper if it's an evening rehearsal as is common in most training institutions). It is common to see an actor's energy flag during a rehearsal because of insufficient sleep or nourishment. When that happens to you, you have only yourself to blame. But your poor work will affect those you work with and the collective work will suffer. So get to bed on time and eat sensibly. As an actor your body is your instrument—respect it. Treat it properly and it will do what you need it to. Punish it and it will fail you, help you to fail, help you to die.

The most common forms of self-punishment actors enjoy are liquor and drugs. Separately or in combination, these can reduce your effectiveness and help you to achieve the failure you seek when you use them. It may be comforting to blame them for your bad performance, but that delusion only lasts a short while. Finally, you know you are doing it to yourself, so that you never need to discover if you are as good as you think you are, as you must be to succeed. The blame can always be laid on the bottle and the joint. "Man, if I had been straight, I would have been terrific" is the empty rationalization of the actor who has so little respect for his work, for the theatre, for his fellow actors, for his audience, and for his very self that he will do almost anything to delude himself.

Liquor is essentially a depressant. For the first shot or so it is a stimulant, but swiftly the muscles lose their edge of coordination, the mind loses its ability to concentrate, the sense of time and the judgment of distance become impaired. In short, the very controls you need to act are debilitated. All the lies about "It's just to relax my throat," "It gets me warmed up," "This much doesn't even affect me," are just that—lies. *If you drink—don't act!*

A drink *after* a rehearsal is wonderful. I'll race you to the bar. But I know I have a full night's sleep ahead and my body will have a chance to recuperate. And I'll be able to respect the work I do the next day. But to arrive at work with a glow on—well, that's just plain stupid.

The most common kind of drug is marijuana and it is also the only kind I can speak of from personal experience. Its purpose, and indeed the primary purpose of most popular forms of drugs, is to adjust the sensory and temporal controls of the mind. Well, it must be obvious that to do so is to render your work useless. Have you ever been on stage with someone who was loaded? I have. It was awful. Suddenly there were long pauses which he believed were either significant or not so long as I and the audience knew them to be. Suddenly there were changed line readings—the result of some associative mental image that was unrelated to the action being played.

A major trouble with using drugs during the rehearsal period of a show is that the effects of the chemical may not be sufficiently short-lived. The temporal and sensory adjustments might not go away with a short nap. Watch out for that.

Among my actor acquaintances is a gentleman who remains loaded most of the time he's not working. I find him very boring at such times, but I try to be tolerant. After all, he's a friend. But from the moment he signs a contract he's Mister Straight Arrow. A clear-headed, well-focused, efficient, working actor. I have engaged him repeatedly and would again.

It is not my intention here to moralize, to tell you how to live your life, or to explicate the complicated laws of our society in relation to drugs and alcohol. It *is* my intention to urge self-respect upon you. To remind you it is achieved through meeting professional challenges, not through avoiding them. You may be very successful and totally dissolute. Others have been before you. But they were never the actors they might have been. I worked once for a director who was drunk most of the rehearsal period. The show was a failure. The experience was an unpleasant one for audiences and actors alike. And I do not believe the man had any self-respect.

One final caution. Don't believe you'll fool anyone. If you're drunk or spaced, the director will know. Maybe not the first time, but he'll learn fast. And when he does, you'll be on your ear. Not just from your present employment, but from any subsequent show he—or the stage manager, playwright, designer, producer, or "gofer"—might be working. You'd be startled at how fast your reputation can precede you. A reputation as a drunk or doper will find you out of the profession and back in your father's grocery business fast.

The theatre is a social art, one that requires people to work together under extreme pressure. The norms of society are mirrored in the working situation and the rules that apply for success in most walks of life apply for rehearsals. You can help yourself if you remember how to behave.

The Political Structure

You're in rehearsal—in the intense quiet of a darkened, sequestered room. There's only the director, the stage manager, the playwright and the other six actors. Here is where it all happens. Where the creativity flows. Where the play is made. Nothing else matters.

If you believe that, it is no wonder you have a strange view of the theatre. As an actor, you seldom see the others who are working every bit as hard as you are. You're wrapped up in the harmonious and fertile crucible of rehearsals and need have no other concerns. You believe you are the advance guard, the infantry that will combat the enemy of the audience, and you may forget that outside, beyond and notably above the rehearsals there are many professionals working at fever pitch to insure the production's success. You are not alone.

Outside the rehearsal room there is an entirely different world. A world of business. And whenever you cross into it, you ought to know about it. You ought to know the people who work in it, the jobs they perform, their relationship to you, your obligations to them, and your place in the huge machinery that is a production company.

The production company is a business with offices and officers and follows the basic principles that guide all businesses. Its intention is to turn a profit or, if it is a not-for-profit company (an institutional theatre), to balance its books. It is an organization that deals in money, although the production it is marketing is a service instead of a commodity. You are a very small part of the company, not much more important to the business's success than the exhaust system on a new Buick is to General Motors. The Buick needs an exhaust system, but if one doesn't function well, another will replace it. General Motors goes on. The production company needs you, but it will continue to do business if it has to replace you. Inside that rehearsal room you may seem essential to the company, but inside the producer's office you are not.

Your relationship to the company is best illustrated by the representative flow chart for a theatrical production company. Some variant of this flow chart exists for every production you work in. If you're a member of a resident theatre the configuration may vary slightly and in a university or training school there may be additional differences. I've also included a flow chart for Temple University's department of theatre and for the Virginia Museum Theatre to illustrate some of the possible differences. But certain truths apply in all these charts and they are important for you to keep in mind.

First, recognize that more people are engaged in mounting the production than performing it; members of the administrative staff, marketing staff, design, construction, and backstage staff outnumber the performers heavily. Next, note the place of the actor on the flow chart—at the bottom. This does not mean the actor is the least important member of the company, necessarily. It means that the actor is the least important in regard to administrative and financial and artistic decision-making. Simply, nobody consults the actor about anything. The actor is engaged to act. His opinions and preferences about operating policy are unwelcome and irrelevant. When you have absorbed these truths, you will find you are happier in your work. All the energy you might direct to worrying about the poster campaign, the number of preview performances to give, the colors for the gels and the number of overtime hours to rehearse can be directed towards your own work. You will be freed to act.

As an actor you have five members of the company you must go

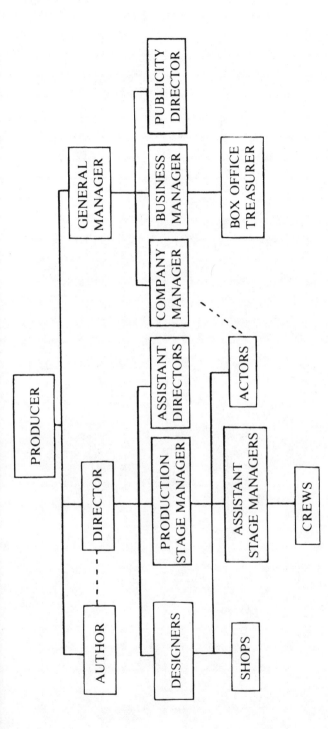

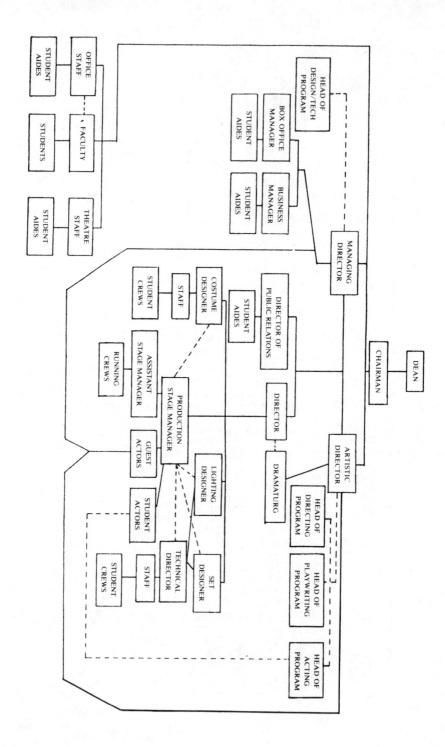

through when you have needs. The director will attend to your artistic needs; the production stage manager will attend to your needs in relation to your working conditions in both rehearsals and performances; the company manager will attend to your business and personal needs; the publicity director will attend to your photographic, press, and program needs; the equity deputy will be your liaison to the producer about extraordinary problems relating to your working circumstances. Don't go to anyone else with your problems unless you are directed to do so by one of these five. If you need house seats for your agent, go to the company manager, not the box office treasurer. If you need a pocket in your costume, go to the production stage manager, not the costume designer.

Each of these five has a direct channel to you—and you have the same direct line to them. Everything you need to know will be told you by one of these five, and every question you might have should be directed to one of them.

Once you have learned the political structure of the company that has employed you, once you know both the people and the jobs, you will begin to perceive the unique nature of the company. You'll find out who is strong, who has taken on tasks not traditionally a part of his job, who gets things done, who is hopelessly overworked. You will begin to learn those deviations from the standard political structure that might affect you; you will begin to learn who on the production has the "muscle." (Unquestionably the finest discussion of this aspect of the actor's world is found in the chapter entitled "Muscle" in William Goldman's *The Season*. The dates and names in that extraordinary book may now be a bit out of date, but the essential work remains invaluable.*)

☆ ☆ ☆ ☆ ☆

Sexual politics exist in the theatre just as in other walks of life. You will work best if you are alert to the most common forms of sexual politics and if you guide your paratheatrical activities with an alert eye to their influence on your acting. The myth and

*William Goldman, *The Season* (New York: Harcourt, Brace & World, Inc., 1969).

reality of the casting couch have been discussed earlier, but this is a good place for a few notions about sexual politics in rehearsals and performance.

Freud has taught us that the sex drive is frequently sublimated into other drives. The drive for wealth, military and political power, religious authority, intellectual superiority, and public acclaim may be surrogates for the sexual drive. Inversely, a position of superiority or authority is frequently expressed through sexual acts. The boss has his secretary, the senator his aide, the rock star his groupies. Indeed, some of us are sexually attracted to people in positions of authority.

In the intense and sequestered world of theatre there are many opportunities for the sexual exploitation of a political power. The director can seduce the actress who wants his approval of her acting and will go to any length to achieve it. The actress can seduce her leading man so that he will perform his scenes as she wishes them interpreted. The stage manager can seduce the extra by dangling hopes of an understudy's job. The critic can seduce the playwright with promises of good reviews. The producer can seduce them all with promises of employment.

You have an obligation to yourself, your fellows, and your work to measure how your possible sexual activities might impede your work. And it can be very hard to keep your lusts and your professional aims separate. It is very difficult to discern which motives should guide your behavior, since you can be quite capable of deluding yourself that the exercise of your political muscle is in fact "true love."

The very nature of the rehearsal circumstance obscures our vision and confuses our feelings, even in non-sexual relationships. Jon Jory, Producing Director of the Actors Theatre of Louisville, described to me his years as a guest director around the L.O.R.T. circuit and explained why it was destructive to his social sanity. He would arrive in a city, he related, and know he would be there for three weeks only. The first day he would meet the dozen or so people he would work with and immediately plunge into intense working relationships with them—relationships in which the emotions are high, the nerve endings exposed, the trust imperative. Within a week, the group was very friendly. A year's casual acquaintance had been compressed into one week. And during that intensive week very little contact with the outside world intruded. In the second week people became dear, old friends. Then came the third week. Just as he needed to work most closely with the actors professionally, he and they perceived the imminency of his departure. Both sides pulled back from the relationship, from the friendship. Both sides were striving to protect themselves from the pain of separation that is a necessity of the transient director's life. "It can screw you up," Jon said. "I was glad to get done with it." If your social sanity can be abused by the rehearsal rhythm, imagine what can happen to your love life. If you're playing Ophelia and three days before you open the production you have a huge fight with Hamlet and he moves back into his own apartment, you're going to have a terrible time rehearsing and performing the show. (Although you may find a richer feeling behind the line, "Oh what a noble mind is here o'erthrown.")

Similarly, try not to get involved with your directors. They are charismatic, energetic, mature, forceful, all-knowing, patient, all-caring, and as a result very attractive. What's more, in the heat of the work, they can be attracted to you. Both of you are of the theatre and supremely gifted at self-delusion; you can play the roles of "lovers" with great conviction. But directors spend their public hours being supportive, caring, forceful, witty, and energetic. Privately, they can need someone who will be those things for them when they get home. Do you really have the strength to rehearse and then deal with an adult who can need your domestic but _not_ your creative instincts? Can you leave the rehearsal together and suddenly reverse roles? The strain can be incredible. And beware of opening night-itis. It is a birthing, a delivery. As an actor, you are a child about to be born, bursting with the energy of new life and crying out for a hearing and for attention. The director is the parent who experiences post-partum depressions.

The wisest behavior would be restraint. Wait until the show opens, at least. Then your world will slow down a little, and you can both explore your feelings sensibly. If you still think the director is terrific, get together. In short, try to separate your work from your pleasure. Try to behave so as to insure your best working circumstances and your happiest private life. Avoid the blurring of theatre and life implicit in John Barrymore's oft-quoted response to the interviewer who asked if he believed

Hamlet was sleeping with Ophelia. "Only in the Chicago company," he quipped.

The People With Whom You Work

Come out of the rehearsal room and meet the people with whom you work. There are clerks and craftsmen, administrators and advocates. There is a long list of people each actor will encounter during the rehearsals for a production, and your work will go well and your life will go pleasantly if you know how to relate to your co-workers. Each is a professional, conscientiously doing his job, and each is working under pressure and adverse conditions which equal yours. None is there as your servant or underling. The over-riding principle guiding your working relationships should be *mutual respect.* If you can learn to put aside your insecurity and acknowledge others' importance to the show's ultimate success, you will do well.

ACTORS   The greatest percentage of your time will be spent with your fellow actors. If you will think for a moment what you need from them to help you do your job well, then you will be able to itemize what you must do to help them—you will learn how to behave with your fellow actors.

Respect their work habits. They are frequently strangers to you and it is safe to assume a great many will go about their work in ways quite different from yours. You need only to watch a play in performance to know the truth of this. Each performer has developed his own variant upon the myriad of methods of acting which are presently taught in the English-speaking theatre and one of the distressing truths about our work is that we rarely create a cohesive production because the actors have no common approach to their work. Have you ever seen the film of Shakespeare's *Julius Caesar* that features Marlon Brando, John Gielgud, James Mason, Edmund O'Brien, and Louis Calhern? There are brilliant performances given by all the name players, but each appears to be in a different play. The same applies to the fine film of O'Neill's *Long Day's Journey Into Night* in which it seems the tortured members of the Tyrone family have never met one another. Each has a different accent, rhythm, appearance, and style of performance. You have no control over the selection of the actors with whom you must work and no way of anticipating how each works. If you are flexible, however, you will not only aid your fellows but you may learn ways of working (techniques of the craft) which you may wish to incorporate into your future work. Let's say that an actor comes to you before one day's rehearsal and says, "I hope you'll go along with this. Today, during the first run of the scene, I want to concentrate hard on the physical realities of the environment: climate, time of day, that sort of thing. Oh, I'll be right with all the lines and business, but don't be disturbed if my concentration doesn't seem to be on you, as it has been." Can you handle that? He's giving you the skeleton of what is needed to get through the scene, and he's obviously bringing to the rehearsal the results of his homework, and he's giving you the chance to work on what you need to work on, and he's giving you a demonstration of a technique that you might one day wish to explore. Can you handle it?

Don't injure your own work habits, on the other hand. Don't be so cooperative that you never get your own work done, that your rehearsal time is poorly spent. The major conflict of interests in regard to the use of rehearsal time will probably not come between you and another actor, but between you and the director. And his preferences will normally prevail, so you must learn to be flexible if you are to accomplish your own ends. For example, if you are an actor who likes to learn the words and the basic moves within the first few days, so that you can forget those external concerns and get to what you feel is the heart of your work—if you're like Olivier, as Peter Brook described him, an actor who achieves his freedom only after the tongue muscles have been externally conditioned to say the correct words—and the director decides to spend the first seven rehearsals improvising the offstage scenes referred to in the action, what will you do? What you cannot do in rehearsals, do at home or during rehearsal hours in some other space. Spend your offstage rehearsal hours and your at-home rehearsal hours doing what *you* need to do. And learn as much as you can from the exercises the director is pursuing. Actors waste a vast amount of their available rehearsal time just sitting around. Not "waiting to go on," just sitting around bored. You ought to use that time to advantage. If you can find an actor you play a scene with, go to it in the hallway, basement, or rest room. Even if you have to work alone, work. If you have a particular order to your own rehearsal process, stick to it. You will profit from the company's joint effort as often as it corresponds to your needs. But when that luxury is denied you, you can still work in your own manner and at your own tempo.

Never give another actor unsolicited advice! Don't suggest how he might say his line, pick up his cigarette, or bring forth real tears. Don't explain to him what the director has just said. Respect the actors you work with by letting them do their work while you do yours. This is a common fault of young actors, particularly those trained in universities where some sort of "let's all get together and do a play, guys" mentality has prevailed. They step beyond their actor's job and naively assume they are directors. Or at the least, they think they are in some summer camp conclave where everyone's opinions are equally important. But the theatre is not a democracy. Egalitarianism does not obtain. The director talks with each actor individually. What is true for the star is not true for you. You don't want others telling you how to do your work, and you must respect them by restraining your impulse to advise them. You may believe you are speaking for the common good, but it is widely thought to be very bad manners for one actor to coach another. Frequently a seasoned veteran will snap at a beginner who breaches this code of conduct, and I've seen tears, wasted energies, and wasted rehearsal time result from just such a social blunder.

Occasionally you will find an actor who asks for help. Be careful; he is probably only asking to be told he's wonderful. Most actors don't want advice, only praise. If you can determine that your compatriot really wants help, then offer it delicately. You might try describing some occasion in which you wrestled with a similar problem. "Yeah, crying is hard for me, too," you might hear yourself say. "I've tried everything from putting soap under my fingernails and then squeezing it into my eyes to trying to remember how I felt when I learned I was going to be divorced. I'm not much good at it. How are you working?" By revealing your own limitations first and then returning the ball into his court, you've initiated reasonable, craft-level discussion. If you can be of help to the actor, great. But don't ever seem to be condescending.

Don't ever boast, "Oh, I've learned how to do that one. You see, what you do is. . . ."

On occasions you will need an actor's help. Perhaps what an actor is doing is keeping you from achieving the quality you are striving for in a given scene. That can happen on a simple, technical level, or on a profound, interpretive one. You may simply need him to come in with a quick cue so your transition to your next beat will fall right, rhythmically, or you may need him to play a very different action in a scene if your characterization is to remain consistent. The first of these problems can be dealt with between actors. Broach the subject by seeking mutual help. "Listen, I'm having trouble with this moment. Can you figure out what I might do here?" More often than not the actor will provide an answer that changes what he does, and thereby makes your joint scene go properly. You will have accomplished your own ends diplomatically. If a major interpretive issue is at hand, raise the subject with the director, using rather the same attack. "Here I am, Lady Anne, on my way to bury my husband, and Richard interrupts me. I have to resist his advances. Well, I find I'm having trouble doing that, because I don't feel he's really advancing. What do I do?" Then the director can do what he's been trying to do for several weeks, namely to correct Richard's false interpretation of the famed wooing scene.

And sometimes you just have to be assertive, though that should come only after you've tried evey polite and diplomatic device you know. I was playing Benedick in *Much Ado About Nothing* and had trouble with a short scene late in the action. Benedick has formally challenged Claudio to a duel and is happily returning to tell Beatrice what he's done and to woo her. He encounters Margaret, young Hero's confidante, who tries to flirt with him. I understood my action: to get to Beatrice. The impediment was Margaret, and the way of overcoming it was through wit, through badinage. It was, I felt certain, a scene to be played swiftly. But the actress doing Margaret knew this was one of her largest scenes in the play and wanted to go slowly, to show the audience her stuff, I suspect. I tried discussing it with the actress. No change. I discussed it with the director, who agreed with me. We worked on the scene, then did a run-through. No change. I spoke with the stage manager and she spoke to the actress. No change. I knew the scene played swiftly was charming and witty and kept the drive of the latter portion of the show going. I knew that the scene played slowly was uninteresting and irrelevant. What to do? I started playing it at the correct tempo. That meant I'd begun my next speech before Margaret had concluded hers, my cue. And, after an appropriate beat, I went right on to my following speech. In a moment she was all in a muddle, unable to get a cue, or hear herself, or play the scene. "Sorry," I told her, "but that's how I've got to play this scene. I hope you have time to get your lines in." She did, in every subsequent rehearsal and performance.

"Let me play the lion's part," says that greatest of all ham actors, Bottom the Weaver. Bottom wants to play every role and to tell his friends how to play theirs. Don't be Bottom, for you too might suffer his fate and turn into a jackass.

Respect your fellow actor's working space. Don't lounge in front of him reading, smoking, knitting, chatting, sleeping. If a show is rehearsing in a small room in which the director's table is only a few feet from the edge of the playing area, never intrude into that space. Don't clutter the working space with your belongings or yourself. If the rehearsal is in a theatre, stay out of the front part of the auditorium, where the working actors can see you—where their concentrations can be shaken by your presence. Don't walk from the waiting area to the playing area along a path that intrudes on the working actor's concentration. Acting is hard enough to do without some unthinking clod marching about before you.

I was directing a show recently in which the most extraordinary breach of this etiquette occurred. The scene was an office with two basic areas, a desk area and a lounge. The play called for an intense scene between two central characters around the desk while a group of characters in the lounge watched the TV and made occasional remarks which provided an editorial counterpoint to the main dialogue. During one rehearsal, as I concentrated on the dialogue scene stage left, I kept hearing low conversation from the other side of the stage. I discovered that one of the actors was going over his dialogue and business for yet another scene in the play. He was not playing his action for the scene being rehearsed (which was to study the TV program), and he was disrupting the other actors' work. When I discovered what was going on, I erupted angrily and berated him for his lack of sensitivity, his poor professional behavior, and his idiocy.

Respect your fellow actor's time. When you are working you wish and need the director's and stage manager's full attention. When your fellow actors are working, they need it. Don't intrude on the concentration of anyone who is at work; don't waste their precious time. Whatever you have to ask the director can wait until an appropriate break in the rehearsal.

Be on hand when your turn to work comes. Don't be in the coffee shop, the tobacconist's, the costume shop, or the rest room. Be alert to the rehearsal's development and be prepared to make your entrance when your scene comes up. Your mutual enemy is time. Join to defeat it.

Respect the seriousness of your fellow actor's work. Don't give in to any childish or childlike impulses. Don't play pranks. It is true that a portion of acting is "playing" and that one of the things that makes you an actor is the exuberance you have. But don't disrupt serious work to gratify your private, non-theatrical needs. Can you rehearse Maggie's opening monologues from *Cat on a Hot Tin Roof* if someone has drawn a smiley-face on the mirror you must use? Or can anyone effectively rehearse the Gwendolyn-Cecily tea scene if you have replaced the sugar cubes with bouillon cubes. Don't denigrate an actor's work by playing silly pranks. That's the stuff amateur theatricals are made of—not a part of mature, professional behavior. (For a delightful and rich discussion of amateur theatricals, read Michael Green's *Downwind of Upstage, The Art of Coarse Acting.**)

Respect another actor's warm-ups and pre-entrance preparations. A brilliant young actor I know goes through the entirety of his role, on stage, before every performance. It sometimes takes him hours. You'll rarely encounter such a zealot, but if you do, respect him. What he's doing is no more extraordinary than what you do. If an actor you're working with spends five minutes vocalizing before each rehearsal begins, let him. Don't intrude on that time to ask about your scene with him. What he is doing is a portion of his working habits and merits your consideration. It's

---

*Michael Green, *Downwind of Upstage, The Art of Coarse Acting* (New York: Drama Book Specialists [Publishers], 1980).

what he needs to do. Don't be guilty of judging its value. You have no grounds for such a judgment.

Nowadays we seldom encounter hard and fast Actors Studio-trained actors, but if you work with such a performer, be alert to and respectful of those working habits. I engaged an actress once, a member of the studio, who made it very clear she was not to be called by her own name once a rehearsal had begun, as she wanted to think, feel, and respond only as the character. You may share my belief that "that way madness lies," but she's entitled to her beliefs and practices every bit as much as you're entitled to yours. There is no correct way to achieve results as an actor and you must be tolerant of whatever habits, warm-ups, and pre-entrance preparations your fellow actors do. After all, as Jerry says in *The Zoo Story,* "Sometimes you have to go a long distance out of your way in order to come back a short distance correctly."

When you are rehearsing scenes of violent action, you must be especially careful of your working manners. Here you may not merely offend a colleague, you may break bones, theirs or yours.

Work slowly. Resist the impetuous actor and the foolish director who urge performance before you're ready. A scene of violence, whether it is brief, like Willie Loman's slap of his son Biff, or complicated like the Mercutio-Tybalt fight, must be rehearsed long and carefully. Both actors must respect the other's needs and work cooperatively. And such scenes ought to be worked outside regular rehearsal hours, as often as you can get together with your partner.

Think of each fight as a piece of choreography. You must know and be able to execute each move in the struggle as precisely as a dancer knows and executes a figure of dance. Fights are commonly staged with beats which can be counted as precisely as dance steps are counted, and you must work cooperatively with your partner to insure a smooth and effective sequence.

You should resist any direction which asks you to use weapons with which you are unfamiliar, unless there is ample time to learn the staging and unless there's a competent fight director assisting you. Do so by explaining that you are worried about hurting your fellow actor. Good stage fighting, as the English fight director B.H. Barry suggests, should not be a risk to anyone. It should be a cooperative venture that gives the illusion of violence, when in fact the activities are all conceived to be mutually supportive for the actors. (Example: I place my hands around your throat and you put yours around my wrists. I struggle to pull my hands *away* and you struggle to *hold* them close to your neck. The tension of our muscles working against one another gives the illusion of violence, but the real actions are in no way dangerous. If I succeed, I break the hold. If you succeed, you can relax your struggle and keep my hands from hurting you.)

If the scene uses weapons or props, you should insist on having the real objects to deal with at the earliest possible moment. That way you can work with your partner carefully, knowing what happens and in what sequence.

The major dangers in scenes of violence come from insufficient rehearsal time of over-zealous actors. The first of these is no doubt behind the English superstitions surrounding *Macbeth*. English actors frequently will not mention the name of the play, instead referring to it as "the Scottish play," and quoting lines from it in the dressing room is taken by many to be bad luck. It is also believed that some terrible accident will occur during any production of the play. Frequently this is explained by alleging that the invocations spoken by the witches are real, but the more sensible reason is this. The play is frequently introduced into the seasons of two-week rep companies when business is flagging. The script is short and can be learned swiftly, and the play usually draws well at the box office. But producing *Macbeth* in two weeks is asking for trouble. All those fight scenes! Small wonder there are many accidents!

You have no control over the selection of the play or length of rehearsal time, but you can help yourself and your other actors by observing sensible professional behavior in the preparation of fight scenes. Don't let someone's exuberance intrude on sound working habits. At the Oregon Shakespearean Festival, as a young actor, I had an upstage scene in the middle of a large battle. My partner and I were to execute what Michael Green calls "the eternal parry " by following a carefully choreographed pattern of blows and counters. My partner was new to acting, much enamored of a misunderstanding of the Stanislavsky system, and liked to believe he *was* his character. In the midst of the battle, as I was dutifully counting 1-2-3-4 and 1-2-3-4, he would forget the rehearsed pattern and come for me! One afternoon I simply stepped aside and swatted him with the flat of my sword, as hard as I could on his thigh, raising (I learned later) an ugly welt. "You see," I explained, "we must follow the pattern as carefully as though it were dialogue. That way I can avoid hurting you." The fight went well from the welt onwards.

☆   ☆   ☆   ☆   ☆

Not all the actors you work with will be humans. Some will be our friends from the animal kingdom. Your way of working with animals, your behavior to them, is an important portion of your entire comportment as an actor. It can also have an immense impact on your effectiveness in performance.

If you are to play a scene with an animal that is unfamiliar to you, request some expert advice. If you're in *Oliver* and must follow the trained dog across a scaffolding to seek out the hidden Bill Sykes, learn as much as you can about the dog from its trainer. If you must carry a chicken across the stage, as I did once in *My Three Angels,* talk to a farmer about the best way to carry a chicken. (I didn't. I tried to keep it upright under my arm, like a football, and got pecked repeatedly. Had I grabbed it by the feet and carried it upside down it would have become a hypnotized, calm, and cooperative actor.)

Just as you must get along with human actors offstage, you must spend time offstage getting to know your animal-actor. This is particularly true if you are a bit afraid of the animal. A young actor I know was engaged by the Disney people to play in a TV western; he lied and said he rode horses well. He was flown from Hollywood to the location in Kanab, Utah. His first shot of the working day required him to mount, ride about 200 yards into the distance, and then ride past the camera, as though he were en route somewhere. He was terrified of horses but in love with paychecks, so he gamely mounted and rode off toward the distant starting place. But the horse bolted and ran amuck, knocked over two expensive cameras, and scattered people and gear until it was captured, with the actor hanging on for dear life. He received a bus ticket back to Hollywood for his pains. The moral: talk to horses. Had he taken the trouble to befriend that horse instead of revealing his fear of it, he might have gotten away with the scene. He might not have been fired.

Animals need a lot of rehearsal time because they are, as a

rule, not as bright as human actors. You will reduce your animal partner's anxieties if you repeat the actions from rehearsal to rehearsal with great consistency. Newness confuses animals. Improvisation encourages catastrophe. You may be bored doing a scene a particular way, but the dog at your side is loving the security of knowing what to do. Don't flirt with danger.

Try, as best you can, to anticipate the audience's reaction to the animal, so that you can be prepared to assist the animal in performance. If, for example, you're doing Launce in Shakespeare's *Two Gentlemen of Verona* and you know the audience is going to howl with laughter at your dog Crab, ask the director to have the company laugh a lot during Crab's scenes, so he gets accustomed to the idea and doesn't grow frightened and lift his leg against yours in the middle of opening night—or worse, so he doesn't start barking at the braying audience.

Not all experiences with animals can be anticipated and there are no guidelines to help you with the unpredicted. You're on your own when they happen. Bats may swoop from the grid, moths get hypnotized in a spotlight, stray dogs may saunter through your love scene, pigeons may drop on your doublet, and crickets may accompany your soliloquy. The strangest of these, in my own experience, occurred one summer during a performance in Hollywood of an outdoor passion play. Happily, I was in the wings. (I was doing Judas, for Equity minimum and thirty pieces of silver a week.) Jesus and his disciples were on stage. Suddenly, an immense and unattractive spider entered from the other side of the stage and casually worked his way toward Our Saviour, whose blood had rushed from his face at the sight. Deftly, and with an act of devotion that surely rivaled his namesake's, John the Beloved strode across the stage and placed his sandaled foot on the intruder. Scrunch! And the show went on!

☆　☆　☆　☆　☆

Animals require one kind of treatment. Stars another. Your behavior in a production with a star may differ from your regular behavior. And with good reason.

A star is any performer whose name assures the production will attract an audience. In Hollywood terms, a star is "bankable"— money for production can be wrestled from a studio if a star is featured in the film. For Broadway, a star is that person whose name will create a pre-sale big enough to keep the play open for a week or two, should the notices be only so-so, and keep it open long enough to discover whether word-of-mouth will build an audience and, consequently, a long run. In stock, a star is anyone whose name will sell tickets. That may well be some TV personality who is not necessarily correct for the role and who may well do a mini-nightclub act following the show to reward his faithful fans. If you are a star, you know it.

Your goal is employment, and to the degree that the star creates the possibility for you to work, the star merits particularly courteous attention. Also, the star is working with a lot more pressure on him than you are. He is certainly playing the leading role, which means he's got more to master than you have—more scenes, more lines, more business, more time on stage to fill with credible acting. It means if the show is a new script trying out, he's got more changes to learn from night to night. It means he has more demands on his time for public relations work. He has to go to TV interviews, do press conferences, have luncheons with entertainment editors. He must give over valuable working time for the purpose of promoting the economic venture which is paying your salary. He must lose additional working time being social with the show's backers—the angels who have capitalized the production. And he has the extraordinary pressure of delivering a performance that is good enough to merit the name he has earned over the years, good enough to carry the show, to live up to his own reputation. You see, under adverse conditions and with extreme pressure on him, the star must do more than merely act the role well; he must be the figurehead, center of morale, and touchstone for the entire venture. Anyone who does all that merits an adjustment in your work habits; after all, your employment depends on the star's success. If he succeeds, you eat, even if your performance is only mediocre.

Accommodate your work habits to the star's. I did a show with Tammy Grimes a few seasons back and she began every rehearsal with a speed line run-through of the scene to be worked. I guess she needed it as a way of warming up, focusing her work on the segment of the script to be attacked in that rehearsal, or maybe just as a way of learning the lines. Whatever. I was playing quite a small role and those line run-throughs were of no use to me. But my work habits were of no consequence. We did line run-throughs. And I did my damnedest to do them the way she liked.

Don't be surprised when the star gives you notes. If just any actor were to give you notes, you would be justified in telling him to put the notes in his ear, but the star is concerned with the total success of the show and will frequently become something of a second director on the production—a first director on some occasions. Some stars reportedly give notes after almost every performance. Take the notes. Smile. If the notes contradict what the director has asked you to do, discuss this with the director discreetly and inquire how to proceed. If they make sense, incorporate them into your performance. Usually such notes will relate to the way you give cues to the star, and I've found they usually make sense. Tammy Grimes knew when a fast or slow cue would set up her punch line, and I was delighted to comply. But if there's an issue of major interpretation at stake, go to the director and ask him to resolve it. Don't fight the star yourself. You'll lose, and you'll make an enemy of someone who might help your career. Don't be so filled with "artistic integrity" that you gain the whole note but lose your career.

The star will expect and receive special treatment. Stage management will have a chair for the star, ice water, candy, and a battery operated fan. And you'll get the floor, a break during which to buy your own soda, and you can fan yourself with your script if you're warm. Don't worry about that. If those flatterings are necessary to get a good performance, don't begrudge them. Remember the star's pressures. And if you're ever successful enough to merit such attention, you'll get it. For now, be professional and do your job. And part of your job is contributing to a happy environment. If you complain about the star's special treatment, you're counter-productive, not to mention stupid.

Most stars are pleasant. They're hard-working actors who've achieved their status because they do their work well and they know their work includes creating a good working ambiance. But occasionally you might work with a louse. Someone who is so insecure as to need to make everyone feel inferior to boost his own petty ego. What to do? Stay clear! Don't get in the way, don't contradict, don't compete. This too shall pass. Be thankful you have the job and do it as well as you can without causing any additional sparks to fly.

If you are any good as an actor, if you have any future, somewhere along the line you will work with a star. As you ascend
towards the heights of your profession you will find yourself
playing scenes with actors whose names have always dazzled you.
You'll discover that stars are good actors and bad actors, nice
people and grouches, but always, always stars. Actors who merit
and require your best behavior.

☆ ☆ ☆ ☆ ☆

"Who's going to be Deputy Dawg?" I heard asked on my first
Equity production. The phrase was borrowed from the cartoon
figure on TV and referred to the election of the Equity deputy.
This is a job one of the senior members of Equity will perform on
every production, in every company. It is an important job,
but actors usually make light of it. It is sadly traditional to elect
anyone who is not present. If you go to the toilet at the wrong
time during the first rehearsal, you may be it.

The duties of the deputy are clearly defined in the Equity
handbook. Essentially he is a foreman representing labor (you) in
negotiations with management (the producer). He can help you in
many ways. At the Great Lakes Shakespeare Festival one
summer the producer suggested we should all wear body makeup
for our production of *Troilus and Cresida*. Most of us had deep
suntans and didn't need it. None of us felt we needed to come to
the theatre an hour early for each show to dob that streaky body
paint all over ourselves. Out came the Equity handbook and up
spoke our deputy. The rules forbade the producer's requiring it
unless he provided us, on the premises, with hot showers. The
theatre didn't have them, and we didn't wear it. Hooray for the
deputy.

The selection of deputy should be taken seriously. Vote for
someone who is experienced, who is mature in manner and will
command the management's respect. At Temple University's
Stage Three the actors once elected a deputy who served them
poorly. He admitted frequently to making demands of management which were contrary to the actor's desires and he tried
negotiating separately for himself. As management, I disregarded him almost entirely and that disadvantaged the company
of players. You can behave sensibly in this matter by supporting
the best candidate, not the absent one.

You should go to your deputy with any problems you are having in relationship with management. He may tell you it is an artistic problem and you should go to the stage manager or director with it; he may tell you it is a personal problem and you should go to the company manager with it; he may tell you you don't have a problem and you should shut up and go back to work; or he may tell you others have mentioned the same concern and that he'll act upon it. If, for example, the director is frequently holding you five or ten minutes at the end of the day, and is doing the same with others, it is the deputy's job to discuss this with the stage manager and either see that the proper hours are observed or that the actors are compensated for the additional time. Your deputy is an actor, like you, and can help you through some of the rough times on the job. Support him, befriend him, and respect him for the services he renders you.

☆ ☆ ☆ ☆ ☆

Remember when you took your clothes off in that hotel room and agreed you would do the nude scene? Well, now it's time to rehearse it. How will your fellow actors behave? How would you behave if one of them were about to "take it all off?" Nudity in public makes most of us pretty nervous and as a result we sometimes behave stupidly. Here are some notions on behavior for the rehearsal of nude scenes which may help you through your first experience.

We are all a mixture of socially and culturally conditioned taboos and childlike desires to be exhibitionistic. That is part of what identifies us as actors. We want to show off our bodies and we are afraid to show off our bodies. This conflict within ourselves causes us to behave uncertainly in any circumstance in which the conflict between the desire and the taboo is made public. Rehearsals of nude scenes are just such situations.

Happily, there is much truth to the homily "familiarity breeds contempt." The more we look at bodies, the less they seem extraordinary. Doctors manage to confront nudity all day long and perform as professionals. So can actors, once they have looked at nudity all day long—or often enough that the novelty has worn off and they can return to the professional tasks before them, the playing of their actions. Think of such plays as *Hair* and David

Storey's *The Changing Room.* Whatever uncertainty of behavior might have affected the casts at the beginning reheasals was surely absent by the time those shows were ready for public viewing.

It is the first few nude rehearsals that create the tension. The sooner in the rehearsal period these occur, the better will be the subsequent rehearsals. If you have a nude scene to perform, ask the director when he would like to introduce this element of the show into rehearsals. It ought to come after you have learned the scene sufficiently so that the scene can be played straight through without stops for prompts, discussion, and coaching. That way the initial "exposure" can be a brief one and you can dress and get on with your work without undue dwelling on the nudity. Certainly you should work nude well before the dress rehearsal, as that normally comes too late in the rehearsal period for you to get over your nervousness sufficiently in advance of opening night.

If you are doing a nude scene, make certain that your costume is presentable. Bathe! Dirty feet on a nude body can be as disruptive to a rehearsal as inappropriate clothes on a costumed one. If the nude body seems inappropriate to the given circumstances of the scene, credibility will be broken and you will have a difficult time playing the scene. Additionally, the actors who play the scene with you will be distracted by the inappropriateness and will begin to focus on you, instead of on your character. That will impede progress unnecessarily.

Bring some sort of robe or covering with you, so that you can be clothed before and after the scene. That way, you'll support the notion that the character is nude, but that you, the actor, are not. Also, you'll help prevent yourself from catching a cold in the poorly heated rehearsal hall.

Try to hold down your exhibitionistic impulses. As a way of covering your nervousness you might employ overkill and parade around in the nude, luxuriating in your "freedom." (I've seen this happen.) All you succeed in doing is making the rest of the company as uneasy as you are. That's disruptive rather than constructive.

As you rehearse the scene, focus on the given circumstances. Your nudity ought to be as appropriate to the scene you're playing as tails would be in a Noel Coward play. If you are playing your actions correctly, you'll reduce initial uneasiness.

Ask the director if you might rehearse the scene a few times with only the actors who are in the scene present—until the novelty has worn off for them and they and you can play the scene without undue self-consciousness. Then, when the actors, crew, and production staff return to the rehearsal hall, you have a degree of self-confidence in yourself, your fellow actors, and the scene which will make it easy for you to go about your work productively.

If an actor other than you is to do the nude scene, you can help by going about your business knowing the actor's skin is the appropriate costume worn for the scene. Relate to the nude actor as you ought to in the context of the scene's given circumstances. Are you, as your character, shocked by it, excited by it, indifferent to it? Play the action of the scene as truthfully as you can and keep your attention on the character, not the performer. As yourself, relating to your fellow actor before or after the scene, refrain from the temptation to make witty remarks.

In all your dealings with your fellow actors simply remember to employ the Golden Rule. Do unto other actors as you would have other actors do unto you.

STAGE MANAGERS   After the actors, you will spend the largest part of your time with the show's stage managers. The production stage manager, so-named because he joins the production in its earliest stages of development, well before the actors are engaged and the rehearsals begun, and because he is the chief authority for running the production through rehearsals and performances, may have a number of stage managers assisting him. On a large musical he may have as many as four assistants. The ranking of the company's stage managers will become evident to you immediately. The production stage manager will delegate responsibilities to his aides, he will convene and terminate rehearsals, he will conduct all "business" during rehearsals (announcements of fittings, changes of scheduling), and he will take primary responsibility for the prompt book, that "bible" of the developing production which will govern the show through its performances. As the chief of his division of the production team (and it is a large division which includes you), he merits your respect and cooperation. So do all the stage managers. They are there to make it possible for you to do your job well. You need them.

There are four phases to the stage manager's work and you need to understand these. The first is the pre-rehearsal period during which much of the play's formative work is completed: concepts are achieved, re-writes undertaken, designs approved, and personnel engaged. It is only in this final area that you may encounter the stage manager. When you come to auditions you are likely to meet an assistant stage manager taking names and giving out scripts. In the audition room you may meet the production stage manager collecting photo/resumés or reading the speeches of other characters for your cold reading. During this first portion of the stage manager's work he is very busy with his job and he is beset by every one of his friends and acquaintances who has learned he's on a show and might help them get employment. What can you do? Be efficient in your use of the stage manager's time, courteous to him for the services he renders (thank him for reading with you), and businesslike in your exchanges with him. If he asks for your phone number don't say you'll get it to him later. Say, "It's SU7-1010, and you'll find it and my service's number on my resumé." Let him know, without being overbearing, that you are a cooperative, responsive worker. You would be astounded at the influence that a production stage manager has on casting. Think of it this way. He's been hired already. The producer and director trust him with what all theatre people know to be a huge and difficult job. They are likely, as a result, to trust his opinion on many matters. If he knows you or is impressed enough by you to commit himself on your behalf, you will be considered seriously. Also, if he is turned off by you, you're through. He need only whisper, "Look out for that one," and your photo will go directly to the circular file.

The second phase of the stage manager's work is the rehearsal phase, the weeks during which the show is shaped. During this period the stage manager is concerned with compiling a correct prompt book, ascertaining all the cues to be called (for lights, sound, fly floor, conductor, etc.), administering the smooth flow of work (seeing that actors get to fittings and photo calls, that props are available for rehearsals), and establishing a healthy spirit within the company. That last item usually means that the stage manager is anxious to keep everyone happy, to head off personality conflicts, and to establish proper discipline from the outset. To do so he may jump on people for tardiness or being slow in learning their lines, and he will attempt diplomatically to guide everyone to a respect for the working space and working process. But mostly he will be your obliging, cheery, and helpful co-worker.

The third phase of the stage manager's work begins the day that full run-throughs begin, which is commonly the day the company moves onto the set, into the theatre. From this moment forward, the production stage manager is the chief executive on the show—even the director takes instructions from him. It is the P.S.M.'s responsibility to make the show run correctly and he has concerns that are larger than those of any other individual. The writer's desire to cut a line must be cleared with the P.S.M. to insure that no cue is affected by the change; only then may the actor be instructed to drop the line. The actor may not decide to sit on the arm of the chair instead of the seat until the change has been approved by the P.S.M., who may be taking a visual cue off the action. (It is at this stage of a production's development that the university-trained actor is frequently confused. In most university situations the stage manager is a student, inexperienced in the position. The director is most commonly a professor and assumes responsibilities which go beyond what a professional director does. As a result, the director frequently runs the final phase of rehearsals, and the student actor learns to ignore the stage manager, who has been shunted to an inferior position by the professor-director's need to get the show ready by opening night. When this happens, the actor learns very poor work habits and may well get confused on his first professional job by the sudden switch of authority from director to P.S.M. I have seen more than one actor being read the riot act by an impatient P.S.M.)

The final phase of the stage manager's work is the performance. Throughout the run of the play the P.S.M. is responsible for the smooth running of the show *and* for the maintenance of its performance standards. That means the P.S.M. is responsible to insure that actors are in the theatre on time, that wardrobe is sent to the cleaners each week, and that the electricians do a nightly check for burnt-out lamps. It also means that he gives notes on the actors' performances and if he feels it essential, he calls brush-up rehearsals. His authority is unquestionable.

As swiftly as you can, learn the P.S.M.'s working habits. Each one you work with will have slightly different habits and if you conform to them you will ingratiate yourself, save valuable time, and contribute to the smooth flow of rehearsals. This will not ask much of you as most stage managers understand they are employed to make your life easy, that they are to be flexible and cooperative, and that your needs are to be respected. That means the stage manager will go 80% of the way. Now, if you'll go 30%, imagine how cheerfully and smoothly things will run.

Right off, learn all the telephone numbers. The P.S.M. will get you a "contact sheet" in the first few days of rehearsal—a sheet with the names and numbers of the company on it, including all important numbers you might need to call. But before it is duplicated and distributed, learn his number(s), the numbers of the rehearsal hall, production office, and wardrobe department. Ask if the stage manager likes being called at home, in case of emergency, and if so, what hours it is safe to call him. He will invariably say "Call me at any hour of the day or night, if it is really an emergency."

Next, learn the rules he enforces at rehearsals. Does he restrict smoking to onstage actions? Does he like all coats and umbrellas left in another room? Does he like you to ask questions about props of him or of the A.S.M.? In short, be sensitive to his working habits and respect them as far as you can without intruding on your own. Yours are finally more important and he knows it. But it is unlikely there would ever be a conflict over honest work habits. Usually, if he requests some change from you, it is the result of his attempt to please one of your fellow actors. So cooperate. If, for example, you wear both contacts and regular eyeglasses, and he asks you to wear your contacts, it may result from the director's remark that the sunlight reflects off your glasses and he can't see what you're doing in your big scene.

Most important is the way a stage manager communicates information. If he makes spoken announcements at the beginning or end of each rehearsal, be certain to be present at those times, to learn what you need to know, and to avoid making him repeat himself. If he posts all notices on a callboard, then check it at your arrival and departure for each rehearsal.

There are many things the stage manager does for you. He will be pleased if you use his services. He's a supplier of writing aides like pencils, scotch tape, note paper, and erasers. He's a supplier of medical aides like aspirin, breath mints, bandages and antacids. He's an aide in line-learning (he'll hold book for you, or find an A.S.M. or fellow actor who will). He'll transmit your needs for props or costumes to the appropriate people (if you need a rehearsal prop, or if your costume ought to have boots tall enough so you can hide a knife in them, tell him). He'll assist you to learn your role by going over line changes and blocking with you—using his prompt book to show you what the correct line or business is. He'll serve as a personnel manager; if you're having a personality conflict with a particular actor, discuss the difficulty with the stage manager. He'll solve 90% of such problems and be happy to be of service. Finally, he'll prompt you during rehearsals. Prompting merits a brief discussion.

The better the stage manager, the better the prompter. A good prompt is given very loudly so that your concentration need not be broken as you strain to hear what's been said. It is given only when you ask for it or when you are obviously stumped. It is always given in a clear and correct manner. A stage manager will try very, very hard to accommodate himself to your habits and needs as he gives prompts. His goal is to help you. There are some ways you can help yourself.

Be consistent in the way you ask for a prompt. "Line" and "yes" are the two most popular requests. The English tend to use "yes" most often. "Line" is most popular in America and seems the less confusing of the two. I've often speculated on the madness that might have arisen during rehearsals for David Storey's *Home* in which many of Sir John Gielgud's lines were "yes." I fantasized an exchange like this in which the initial line is correct and no prompt required:

> JG: I see. Yes.
> PSM: Yes?
> JG: Yes?
> PSM: (mistakently repeating the prompt) *Yes.*
> JG: No. I know. It's "Yes," yes?
> PSM: Yes.
> JG: Oh, I see. Yes.

Well, who could work his way out of that confusion? I prefer and recommend the consistent use of "line." Inexperienced, impetuous, and self-indulgent actors sometimes snap their fingers, or moan "Oh . . . oh . . . oh . . . don't tell me . . . oh. . . ." Rude actors say things like "dammit." All such manners are undesirable as they confuse the prompter and offend your fellow actor.

Don't ever ask for a repeat of your incorrect delivery of the line. Don't say "What did I say just then?" A good prompter will *never* repeat your error, so as not to support it in your mind or ear. He'll only give you the correct line. You'll confuse everyone and stall the rehearsal by asking to hear spoken back to you lines which are not in the text and which can only confuse you and the actor whose cue is your correct line.

There are some things you can do to help the stage manager. Never interrupt the stage manager while he's working. Wait for a break in the rehearsal. You may not think he's doing anything as he sits over his prompt book watching a run-through, but he's working. Perhaps he is counting the seconds in which a scene shift must be prepared or a costume changed. Whatever, respect his work. You don't want him stopping your scene to discuss lighting cues, so don't you stop his work to inquire about your needs.

Instruct the stage manager of anything you learn about the flow of performance which relates to your work and that he will need to know. For example, if you have only twenty seconds of dialogue and a ten-second scene shift in which you must cross to the other side of the stage, change costume, beard, and grab the leash on a pack of bloodhounds, you're going to need assistance. Tell the P.S.M. and he will build that off-stage maneuver into his production plan and you will get the help you need. Less dramatically, if you need to have a prop off-left and the actor who handles it before you leaves it off-right on her exit, tell the P.S.M. and he will arrange to have it where you need it. Or, if the low volume of a line makes it impossible for you to hear your entrance cue, tell the P.S.M. so he can arrange a way to insure you get your cue. The P.S.M. takes pride in a well-run show, and he will appreciate your help. He'll be unhappy with the actor who whines and snivels, "I can't hear my cue," "I can't make that change," and "Somebody lost my prop." But he'll want to work often with the actor who notifies him during rehearsals of the problems that may arise and courteously asks for assistance.

Keep the stage manager notified of your whereabouts during

rehearsals. If you are working somewhere else in the rehearsal complex, or if you are at a PR or costume call, make certain the stage manager knows about it. You can save him aggravation and time wasted looking for you.

Respect the stage manager's rules. He sets them with an eye to keeping everybody happy and the show running smoothly. If you like to smoke and he has asked everyone not to, don't. Which do you place more highly? Your work or your personal habits? If it is the latter, don't be surprised if nobody wants to hire you.

The stage manager has no time for you when the final phase of rehearsals begins. For several weeks he has joked with you, catered to you, prompted you, maybe even gotten drunk with you. Now there is a sudden shift in his attentions. You are one small and very insignificant part of the show. He's concerned with cues and sound levels, the duration of scene shifts, and the logistical management of scores of people who are working the show—people you've never seen but who are just as important to the show's success as you are.

For a short while your relation to the stage manager must shift from co-worker to boss-employee. He needs you to be present, on time, consistent, cooperative, and above all silent. Do not expect favors from him. Do not be slighted by his seeming disinterest in you. Once the show has opened, if it runs a week or a year, he'll be able to re-engage in his friendly relation with you. For now, he's too busy to deal with you. You can help him and help yourself by knowing this, and by doing your job well. And by being silent. As time is the general enemy of theatre, time and noise are the enemies of those final, complicated, nerve-testing rehearsals.

THE DIRECTOR   "What does your dad do?" the seven-year-old was asked. "He's a play director." "But what does he do?" "Well, at the theatre he tells everybody where to go and what to say and how." From the mouths of babes, the proverb has it, comes wisdom.

The director assumes full responsibility for the "artistic" standards of a play. He's responsible for the designs, as he approves them; for the actors, as he selects them; for the script, as he undertakes to direct it; for the music, the lighting, the tempo, the tone. For the whole thing. One part of his responsibility, perhaps the most visible part, is the performance of the actors. He's responsible for what you do.

The director selects you because he believes that of the actors available to him you are the best. Once he has selected you he has two ways to achieve the desired performance: coach you to do it or fire you and get someone who can. This simple truth ought to lead you to several eyebrow-raising discoveries. The standard Equity contract permits management to fire you during the first five days of rehearsal without paying you a separation fee. If you're retained past five days, you can't be fired unless you're given two weeks' notice (or given two weeks' salary and told you're not needed at rehearsals any longer). That five-day clause is your union's recognition of the basic principle underlying your engagement: the assumption that you can act, can do the job you've been hired to do. When a cab company hires a driver, it is assumed he knows how to drive a car and that if he's given a route, he can reach the assigned destination. It's assumed he knows the traffic rules, is licensed to drive, knows enough to stop for gas when it's needed, and will normally avoid accidents. The actor, it is likewise assumed, knows how to rehearse, how to do his makeup, how to learn his lines, how to behave, and how to reach his destination: a good performance. The actor is expected to know *how* to do his work. All the director will do is tell him where he's headed and attempt to assist him when he makes wrong turns in the road. If the driver can't drive, he's out of a job. The same thing is true for the actor who can't act. This proves a confusion for many young, university-trained actors who are accustomed to their directors being their teachers. In most school situations the director tries to teach at the same time he directs and the student actor unhappily grows accustomed to the idea that the director will help him to act while helping him to meet the challenges of a particular role. This work habit is a tough one for many young actors to break. They come into a commercial situation and are puzzled when the director does not take time to help them—to teach them their craft.

Just as an actor might be replaced if he cannot arrive at a good performance, he might be dismissed if he does not know how to behave. Let's assume an actor is always late, or talks during rehearsals, or interrupts when the director is talking, or disappears on coffee breaks at inopportune moments, or back-bites about everyone's performance, or in other ways displays bad professional behavior. Such an actor might well be let go, as the opening dialogue of this book reveals.

He might just as easily be let go because he doesn't know how to rehearse. He doesn't learn his lines, say. Or he can't do improvisations. Or he can't adjust to changes in blocking. Or he's so clumsy he stumbles over furniture or lets his horse get away from him and it runs amuck through the camera equipment.

If you cannot do the job, you'd be wisest to turn it down. If the role calls for a swordsman who can speak several passages in credible French and you're only at home with Turkish and a switchblade, discuss that with the director before you accept the job. He'll respect you for it, and if he hires you he'll never blame you for what you can't do. He knows the responsibility is his. If he doesn't engage you, be happy. He has demonstrated he likes your acting. He probably will engage you whenever he's looking for your type, particularly because you've earned his professional respect. And you've saved yourself the embarrassment of being fired—as you surely would have been whenever the first fight rehearsal was ended.

Not very many actors are fired, and perhaps I'm guilty of scare tactics here, but my aim in this handbook is to provide guidelines which will help actors to work. As an actor you must understand that the moment you are signed to a contract you are subject to the legal cancellation of that contract. The director's relationship to you should always be seen in this light. In the school circumstance the director-teacher has a responsibility to help you improve during the rehearsal period. In a professional circumstance the director has a responsibility to get a good performance from you. He will try every device his skill and time permit him to try. He won't give up on you hastily, if only because that would cast doubt on his judgment in casting you. But he'll drop you as soon as he's convinced you can't make it.

☆ ☆ ☆ ☆ ☆

The actor proposes, the director disposes. From your study of the script and your homework and your discoveries during rehearsals, you develop your performance, and the director tells you when you're doing well and/or poorly. If he doesn't tell you anything, you may assume that either he is delighted with what

you're doing, or he's willing to accept it since he doesn't know how
to help you to make it better.

Of course, the process isn't so cut and dried, nor so one-direc-
tional. The director will "direct," will tell you what to do: where to
go, how to say a line. When you get specific directions, your task
is to do them, and to make whatever justifications you require in
your internal development of the character's actions which make
those movements and line readings "correct." Sometimes the
director needs you to move to a particular place for entirely
pictorial reasons—your body is part of a visual composition which
communicates to the audience the essential meaning of the scene.
You must find a reason for your character to move to the assigned
place if the director doesn't provide one. Sometimes he needs you
to speak a line slowly, so as to help build the audience's suspense;
the justification for that action is yours to find. The director tells
you what to do and you need to find out how and why. If you're
having a hard time, the director will try to help you. There is, of
course, the old tale about the Broadway director of musicals and
farces who was directing a juvenile trained at the Actors Studio.
The actor was told to cross to the window and look out on a particular line. For days the actor did as told, but felt no justification.
Finally he approached the director. "Sir, I've been doing the cross
just as you told me, but I don't understand it, and frankly I don't
think it's a motivated cross, and could you please tell me my
motivation?" "How about your salary?" retorted the director.

One way to get along with your director is to be prepared for the
day's work. Know what is to be rehearsed. Work on that
particular segment of the play as a portion of your homework.
Come to the rehearsal with your lines, business, actions, images,
and recalls all in order. The actor who wanders into rehearsal
and asks, "What scenes are we doing today?" is ill prepared.

Each director will hold his own kinds of rehearsals and will try
to get from you the individual and group performance he desires
through various methods. The most common forms of rehearsals
are show-and-tell, discussion, improvisation, games, gestalt exercises, speed rehearsals, reading and psycho-physical exercises.
The extent to which a director will employ any of these will
depend on the property being rehearsed, the time available for
rehearsal, the group he's working with, and his own strengths.
For example, I directed *The Member of the Wedding* for The
Virginia Museum Theatre and had just under three weeks'

rehearsal with a cast of actors I'd never seen before. During all that time we did only one improvisation and two rehearsals in which something akin to games was used. All the rest was reading, discussion, and show-and-tell. But during a four-and-one-half week rehearsal period for Strindberg's *The Father* with a company I knew fairly well, we did improvisations almost daily, played games regularly, and explored many rehearsals using recorded sound effects to help establish the desired moods. The director will try to be sensitive to the company's needs and abilities, but finally he will use the techniques he judges wisest. Your task is to work within the framework he establishes. If you have gone through formal actor training you will be experienced with many forms of rehearsal. The more directors you work with, the wider will be your experience of rehearsal procedures. What you owe your director is a willingness to try whatever he chooses—an openness to new techniques that may help you both achieve your ends. If you resist and fall back on your own devices, you will impede the director's and the production's development. Correct professional behavior dictates that you explore all approaches to your work and that you do so enthusiastically.

Most directors give notes. Some write them down and distribute them, others say them to the assembled cast, since most notes affect the work of more than one performer. Write down all the notes that affect you. One sure difference between the professional and the amateur is the seriousness with which directions are heeded—and notes are the most concrete form of direction. The actor with sound working habits writes down all the notes he gets, works on each prior to the next rehearsal, and improves with each day's work. The actor with poor habits listens, remembers what he can, and makes many of the same mistakes rehearsal after rehearsal. Nagle Jackson, then artistic director of the Milwaukee Repertory Theater, was directing a group of students. I asked him what some of their deficiencies were. "Well," he smiled, "I'd forgotten you have to give student actors the same note twice."

☆　☆　☆　☆　☆

One breach of good behavior common to actors is to start directing. This is sure to offend director, stage manager, and actor alike. Yet, many do it all the time—until somone puts the offender in his place. Somehow actors get the mistaken idea that theatre is a democratic art. Perhaps this notion developed from the confusions between lifestyle and theatre-practice which led many in the 1960's to invert the creative process and to begin imitating theatre in their lives. Perhaps it results from the actor's egotistical need to seem an authority on all subjects. Whatever its source, it is offensive behavior. Theatre is a benevolent dictatorship, not an egalitarian commune. The director does not want your suggestions about interpretation, staging, timing, or execution. Either the director knows his business and you're a nuisance with your unqualified suggestions or else he doesn't know his business and is threatened by your suggestions, no matter how honest your intentions. In either case, your unsolicited advice is disruptive to the director, troublesome to the stage manager, and insulting to your fellow actor. When that innocent urge wells up in you to say, "Hey, do it this way," keep your mouth shut!

Similarly, don't direct yourself. Don't stop in the middle of a run-through to discuss the appropriateness of your interpretation or your business. Don't anticipate the director and stop a scene to look out, waiting for his reaction. Act! If he wants to stop you, he will. You are not the only person in a scene, and it may be that the others require continuity more than you need discussion. Regardless, the choice lies with the director, not with you.

Don't start directing others' scenes in the lobby. Restrain your enthusiasm and let the actors do their acting and the director his directing. And you mind your own business. In all likelihood you have more than enough work to do on your own role.

Some directors are bad directors. I have worked for three different directors with Broadway credits who have fallen asleep during rehearsals. I have worked for a director in a resident theatre who, during three weeks of rehearsal for *Escurial,* de Ghelderode's complex two-person play, said only four things to me, one of which was "Could you do the final part faster?" I have worked for directors who have given me incorrect definitions of words that appeared in my speeches. Sad but true, many directors are bad directors. And you need to know how to protect yourself and how to behave toward them.

Begin by knowing when to say "No." There are times when you

must refuse to do what a director instructs you to do. You must never do this for reasons of ego, but for reasons of your intelligence and craft. You must never refuse to execute a move or line-reading because you "feel" it is inappropriate. You must be able to state firmly and clearly the reasons the direction is inappropriate, and you must be prepared to counter with a sensible and defensible alternative. When you are thus prepared you may engage in justified debate and strive to win your point. Don't waste valuable time in endless debate, and don't be a continual talker, but do protect yourself. An example will clarify this notion.

I was playing Macduff. We were rehearsing the final scene in which Macduff confronts Macbeth. "Turn, hell-hound, turn." Macbeth got to "Before my body I throw my warlike shield . . ." and tossed his shield down on the ground. "Ah ha," I thought, "I'll cleave him from his nave to his chops." But the director told me to throw down my shield as well. "No," I said. "I've come here to kill that swine, and now I've a perfect opportunity." The actor playing Macbeth said he threw down his shield because the script had so indicated: "Before my body I throw my warlike shield." "No," I repeated. "If he throws down his shield I will simply chop him into messes. Unless he runs away, which seems hardly in keeping with his warrior-like speech that follows." The director argued that the gentlemanly code of chivalry would require me to throw down my shield if he had thrown down his. I laughed and replied that this was not accurate historically and that the action of Macduff could not be clearer: to kill Macbeth. We debated this for many minutes (the debate was more interesting than the battle we finally staged, I assure you). I was trying to protect myself from what I knew to be a directorial blunder. My argument had nothing to do with me (although I did not relish being laughed at, as I suspected would be the case if we staged the scene as the director was requesting), and a lot to do with my craft. Ultimately, the director said the magic words, "Never mind about all that; I'm the director and do it like I said." I complied, as I was contracted to do. The director is boss, and you must comply with his directions, but you also must assert yourself any time you are directed stupidly—and more often than not, if your "no" is backed with good reasoning, you'll win your point.

Bad directors rarely lead you to confrontation. More commonly, as with the chap directing *Escurial,* they don't do anything, or else they don't recognize that you are taking care of yourself. If that's the case, don't seek confrontation. Try, as best you can, to think through your role beat by beat as though you were in a class doing an exercise. And create the best performance you can. When in doubt about a choice, make the least conspicuous one. Without a good director out front disposing of what you propose, selecting from among the actions you're exploring, it is easy for you to make a choice that will stick out like the production's proverbial sore thumb and make you noticeable to the critics who will hang you by it. Anonymity is the better part of valor.

The director is your friend. In the hours you will rehearse together, across the shows you may do together, you will come to know him very, very well. I count among my warmest friends some of the actors I have directed, some of the directors I've acted for. But those friendships should not intrude into the rehearsal. I don't mean that you both suddenly put on sombre masks and work with austere aloofness. I mean that the friendship must not influence professional judgment. Don't ask to play a role you know you're wrong for. That will only strain your friendship. Don't bring your personal squabbles into the rehearsal. That will only mar your work. Separate your friendly director from your friend the director. Respect both.

THE DIRECTOR'S ASSISTANTS   On large productions the director may have assistants who undertake portions of the direction and who deal with you as though they were directors. Five common types of assistants are the choreographer, musical director, vocal coach, fight director, and assistant director (someone who has no specialty but who has been engaged to work with you while the director works with others). It is common for an assistant director to work with the members of a crowd, for example, or with the chorus in a Greek tragedy. On *Romeo and Juliet* I was fortunate to have a choreographer, a fight director, and an assistant director whose primary task was to coach the leads, particularly in their two love scenes. Fred Adams, of the Utah Shakespearean Festival, once directed *A Midsummer Night's Dream* with one assistant directing the fairy sequences and another directing the mechanicals while he directed the young lovers and the court scenes and supervised his assistants.

(This is a fine way for young directors to get their apprenticeship.) In films it is common for the dialogue director to coach inexperienced actors prior to the camera rehearsals for a sequence.

The director's assistants have specific jobs and the responsibility to help you learn a particular portion of your role. They will relate to you in precisely the same manner the director will and you must strive to cooperate with them fully.

Assistant directors normally have particular talents and are frequently engaged because the director himself is not an expert. You can learn much from the assistant and you will develop a full performance if you apply yourself as rigorously to his rehearsals as you might to the director's. Some additional thoughts: assistants frequently grow up to be directors, and you may further your career by impressing the assistant; assistants necessarily have different personalities and work habits from the director, and you must be flexible enough to work for both without revealing your preferences; the rehearsal time you spend with an assistant is time you might otherwise have wasted, so be thankful for it, not resentful.

How do you behave if you receive contradictory directions? If the musical director, for example, guides you to a harsh and angry singing of a song and the director (in his sessions) keeps alluding to the gentle mood that will follow the song, you're in temporary trouble. You can make things worse if you engage in a squabble. You can make things better if you bring the contradiction to the stage manager's attention, let him bring the two directors together, and let them resolve what the desired interpretation will be. When in the middle, pass the buck!

You'll rarely be in the middle, happily. Typically, the director will lay out his intentions to his assistants quite clearly. Additionally, he will check in on all the sub-rehearsals periodically and will catch any deviations early. But once in a long time you may find yourself the pawn in a power struggle between the director and one of his assistants who is ambitious and believes he might get the director's job if he is tenacious. When that happens, duck! And never take sides. You don't know who's going to win, and you want to keep your job no matter what happens. The stage manager remains your escape hatch. If the director and choreographer are screaming at one another (for the producer's benefit, no doubt), just turn to the stage manager and ask, "Which way do you want me to do it?" He'll get you out of your pickle, and because he's not an artistic decision-maker there's little likelihood he'll fall in any purge that may hit your troubled show. But I'm describing a rare event, one you needn't be concerned about most of the time.

PLAYWRIGHTS   Exciting rehearsals happen when the playwright is at your side. In all rehearsals there is an invigorating fusion of creative energies. When the playwright is among you, re-shaping the event to exploit your particular gifts, the experience is wonderfully dizzying. Your sense of danger is deliciously heightened because you know that nobody has played your role before. There are no paths to follow, only trails to blaze. Your sense of responsibility is great because you know your creation of the role will influence every actor who plays it in productions yet to come. In the most temporal of arts this is your fleeting chance for immortality.

The *genus playwrightus* is an enigmatic being. In the 1960's, heyday of group creativity, some thought he was an endangered species, the potential victim of an ecological shift. Throughout theatrical history he has been both the spokesman of the devil and the darling of the gods. As society has changed, so have its attitudes towards its playwrights. For actors as well, the playwright has an ambivalent status. He's that nitpicking work-maker who fusses over details. And he's that dark visionary who gives our feelings life. In the Italian comedy of the Renaissance he fused with the actors as completely as he does with such contemporary improvisatory actors as those in Boston's *The Proposition* and San Francisco's *The Committee*. In the literary salons of the Roman Empire he banished the actors and proclaimed the ascendency of closet drama. In our own time, and for a long time to come, he is our most exciting co-worker, for he brings us the stories, characters, and actions we play. He merits our respect, love, and tender care.

The rules governing your working relationship with the playwright during rehearsals will be dictated by the director and must be observed by you. Typically, the director will forbid the playwright and actor to talk to one another. You may find this strange, since you have much need of the playwright, but it makes good sense. You cannot be directed by two people at once, and you'll become either schizophrenic or traumatized if you are not protected. The director knows this, and hence sets up a communications link with himself at its center. Anything the writer needs to tell you must go through the director, who can head off any notes that conflict with what he's telling you and can translate into actor–ese any notes that he believes might be meaningless or confusing. Any questions you have for the playwright must go through the director so that he can screen out questions which are his to answer, not the writer's, and so that he can translate into writer–ese any of your requests that might confuse the playwright. If the director knows and trusts the playwright, he might relax this rule, but even so you are well-advised to tread cautiously. Don't get caught between conflicting guides.

The playwright is rarely a good director. Indeed his process of creativity is quite different from yours, and if you understand this, you will see why problems arise. In psychological terms, as Philip Weisman discusses in *Creativity in the Theatre*, ". . . actors often suffer from an undeveloped self-image and intensified conflicts around exhibitionism, whereas the dramatist has the tendency toward enactment (inclusive of acting out), from which he dissociates himself in his capacity as an artist and utilizes its contents for his dramas."* Simply, the urge to express himself leads the actor to public display, but the writer sublimates it into the private act of writing. Think of your preparations for your work. You exercise your body to warm up, jumping about the room, chanting, gibbering, and generally making a spectacle of yourself. Think of the writer's. He withdraws from every external stimulation, finds a quiet space, and directs all his energy toward thinking. The impulse to enactment is translated into the impulse to think—to write down the thoughts. If he is well disciplined, he may have lost his urge to act things out, and he may be a poor judge of how you go about your work. The director knows this, understands the ways in which both of you think and work, and is the necessary link between you. That's why his rule separating you is a wise one that you must observe.

When the director permits you to speak with the playwright, ask him for *information* about the character, the given circum-

*Philip Weisman, *Creativity in the Theatre* (New York: Basic Books, 1965).

stances, and your relationships to other characters. Where was
your character before this entrance? Why do you pick up the
apple, as the script dictates? How many hours have passed
between scenes? What's the temperature in the room? Who is
your closer friend between your brothers? The playwright is the
source of immense amounts of information that you would otherwise have to determine arbitrarily. Your subtext, your grasp of
the given circumstances, and most importantly your motivations,
need not be in doubt. The writer may not have thought out all the
details that you will ask about, and some of your questions may
cause him to lift his eyebrows reflectively and confess, "I've never
even thought about that." But the answer he ultimately provides
is an absolute one, for only he has the full experience of the play.
After all, it came out of him.

Make suggestions about your role and dialogue. These must
never be made thoughtlessly, nor in an attempt to build up the
size of your role. Restrain your ego and apply your craft. Your
request should never begin with "I want." Instead, say "If there
were a different speech here, I could do what the script has me do
in the next scene with greater conviction." You may discover that
the writer has left out a necessary step in your character's
emotional development, and if you draw this to his attention,
you may receive changes that will help you do your job and which
will coincidentally help the audience to enjoy the play. Similarly,
you may discover you're doing things and saying things you don't
need to do or say. Perhaps your subtextual development is
hindered by a speech or an action. Discuss this with the writer.
He may have a textural reason he needs you to do what he's
written, but more than likely he will be delighted to learn that
some cuts can be made—that you can enact what he has only
described.

If you're having real trouble with a particular line or phrase,
you might ask the playwright to re-cast the ideas, to re-phrase
the line. Be careful here that you don't mistake your laziness or
ineptitude for a real problem. Your reason for the desired change
should never be "I can say it easier this way." Actors frequently
confuse their characters with themselves and want all dialogue to
be as *they* would say it. But the writer has not written you. It is
your job to act the character he's written—a character who speaks
as the written lines suggest. In the press of rehearsals, actors

commonly look for shortcuts, and changing dialogue to make it sound "natural" is a common and destructive shortcut. The writer's work must be respected. You're not the writer. So don't try writing your own dialogue. Act his. The greatest offenders here are film and TV actors. In those media, the human emotion in close-up is primary and as a result the actor must seem comfortable. Commonly actors are permitted (even encouraged) to paraphrase. (Writers have usually made some painful accommodation to this practice and are wounded but accepting.) But in stage work, either say the line as it's written or offer the playwright a sound reason for a change. As a rule, don't offer an alternative. Don't try to do his job. Just ask for his help.

Don't talk with the writer about actor problems. Don't discuss with him the imagistic pattern you're using in a scene and don't tell him the emotional recall you're using at your big moment. And never talk with him about your subtext. These are all tools of your craft, as balance, internal rhyme, counterpoint, and imagistic juxtaposition are tools of his. To act the role you don't need to know that the apple is a visual and verbal metaphor for New York, and he doesn't need to know that the recollection of sour milk is what brings that exquisite expression of agony to your face. You see, the director does have to serve as a translator.

Throughout the rehearsal period the writer will fiddle with the script. This will always be done in consultation with the director, but you will be expected to accommodate these changes quickly. It's a part of your job. Many of the changes will be tiny—subtle adjustments of syntax or additions or deletions of phrases that give the script its desired texture. These will not alter your actions, subtext, imagistic pattern, or stage business. Take the changes, learn them, do them. Other changes will be major. In a tryout show you may well be required to play a scene each evening in script "A" while each afternoon you rehearse script "B." When "B" is ready it is then inserted into the performance. On rare occasions there may be four or five variants on a sequence and you may suddenly find you're re-rehearsing "A," since it now is thought superior to the four failed variants. When that happens, you are in a wild and desperate situation. Study hard, concentrate clearly, and do your best. Your best behavior must be displayed in such trying circumstances. Remember, nobody is trying to please you. Nobody cares which way you like to play the scene. The director, playwright, producer, composer, lyricist, and playdoctor are all trying to learn which way the *audience* likes the scene. That's the only measure of appropriateness. Your task is to remain cheerful, cooperative, and hard working.

Rehearsals for a new play breed love and great affection. And yet, the playwright is not your friend. Playwrights tend to be very much like people. There are shy ones and brash ones, pompous ones and frightened ones, battle-weary veterans and newcomers. Their professional admiration for your professional accomplishments will be sincere and their feigned enthusiasm for your inept performance will be phony, and you won't always be able to tell one from the other. Both of you know that the good morale of the company is an essential part of any show's success, so you'll hug each other, compliment each other, buy each other beers, and all this seemingly personal behavior is merely professional manners gone beserk. In fact, you don't know each other and are not friends. You will be drawn to his charisma as the creative center of the project, and you are likely to mistake his public graciousness for private friendship. But opening night will reveal the truth of the situation.

If the show is a flop—he never knew you. If the show is a hit—he returns to his friends, his activities, his private life, and he may never see you again. His work on the show is completed and yours goes on. He may pass you on the street and not recognize you. Don't be offended. You have been an important and wonderful part of his life, and he of yours, but a life in the theatre is made up of time capsules—one for each show you do (or each company you're with). Some few of your co-workers may become your friends, and all become your professional colleagues, but don't be hurt when one doesn't invite you home for dinner. The playwright is probably the first who will remove himself from your daily world. Respect his removal.

SCENE DESIGNER   You may never meet the scene designer. His work is normally completed before you are hired and done in studios and shops far from where you rehearse. You might meet him only if he drops by rehearsals to watch a run-through for the purpose of learning if he needs to discuss any problems with the director (the director has you climbing a trellis that is only decorative and won't support your weight). Or he's on hand when the set loads into the theatre and final touch-ups require his attention. If you have the chance to meet the scenic designer, be friendly. Designers usually like actors. They have little commerce with them and are consequently fascinated by them. You, in turn, can widen your horizons and your contacts by chatting with the scenic designer. (Like the P.S.M., the scenic designer is hired onto a production in its earliest stages, and his opinion is a valued one. I know one actor who was hired on the recommendation of a designer. For every one I know there must be many others.)

You can help the designer by describing to him the way a setting or prop is used in performance, should he not know or should he ask. Don't run up to him panting and tell him what he already knows. Discretion must be employed. Let him introduce the subject.

Don't offer your opinions about his work. I had an embarrassing car ride two seasons ago. I had engaged the director Davey Marlin-Jones from the Loretto-Hilton Theatre in St. Louis and he was staying at my home until he found satisfactory accommodations. He rode with me to the airport as I picked up an actress just arriving to the city and we drove to the theatre together. "Who will be designing the show?" the actress inquired. I told her. "Oh, God," she whined, "his work is so tacky." Davey's eyes turned slowly to me. He had just met the designer and didn't yet know that the man was brilliant, swift, and cooperative, didn't yet know that he was going to be delighted with the setting. The actress's naive and thoughtless remark gave him an unwarranted scare and, worse, it made him wonder what kind of an actress this might be whose behavior was so awful. He later discovered she is a fine actress, but a young and bad-mannered one. She should have kept her opinions to herself; she knows nothing about scenic design. Most actors know nothing about scenic design.

Don't give the scenic designer instructions. If you have a particular problem with the set, talk to the stage manager. It is not your place to give instructions to anyone.

LIGHTING DESIGNER   You may never meet the lighting designer. If you do, it is unlikely his work will be altered because of anything you say or do. You do not interact with him. Your job is to conform to what he has done. His is to achieve what the director requests. The director worries about how the lighting affects you. That's the structure of the working relationship.

You may meet the lighting designer just prior to one of the final or technical run-throughs. If you have arrived early and are checking over the set or some of your business, you may find the lighting designer at work. Introduce yourself. He'll probably already know who you are, as he'll have been watching some rehearsals. Chat with him. You may make a friend, and you can certainly help your performance by learning from him.

Ask him some professional questions. Find out what colors he's gelled the lamps with—that can affect your makeup. Ask him where certain lighting areas drop off—that might guide you to tiny adjustments in your blocking which will keep you well-lit. Ask him if there's anything you can do in your performance to help him achieve the effects he's striving for. Let's say you're Banquo's ghost, and you pop up from a trap door. Let's say there's a large green light directly over your head, which you've never seen. Let's say that by leaning back slightly as you pop up you'll look appropriately ghostly, his lighting will look terrific, and the audience will get a thrill. By behaving professionally, by asking the right questions of the right person, you will have improved your own performance and the total impact of the production.

Don't offer your opinion. If you think the lighting is lousy, keep it to yourself. If you're acting, you're inside the show and can't possibly see what it looks like, so don't offer an unqualified opinion. Even if you're right, why create ill will, make enemies, spread uncertainty through the company, and undermine your collective efforts? The lighting designer is not qualified to judge your acting and you're not qualified to judge his lighting. If both of you are good, fine. You'll both contribute to the show's success.

COSTUME DESIGNER   You will definitely meet the costume designer, and you will meet his assistants: the cutters, tailors, and wardrobe crew who create and maintain the costumes you will wear. These people are of immediate and continued importance to your work and you must behave in a manner that will make you friends. Remember, "Apparel oft proclaims the man." Your visual impression on the stage is mightily significant. Cyrano's nose and Richard of Gloucester's hump are only extreme examples of a continuing theatrical reality—you must appear appropriate if the audience is to believe in you. Sensibly, you must cooperate with those who have a great impact on the way you appear.

The costume designer may have completed his designs before you are engaged, but if your body varies greatly from the director's and costume designer's preconceptions, adjustments will be made (or an entirely new costume designed) to insure that you look right. Once in a long while a designer's rendering will anticipate the actor's appearance uncannily.

You will normally meet the costume designer at an early fitting. During this, and subsequent fittings, you can do much to help him, and he to help you. Give him any information that might affect the developing construction of the costume, anything you may have learned in rehearsals or developed in your work on your role. Are you introducing a particular physical carriage? A limp or a stooped walk? Has the director given you explicit business that the designer may not know about? Do you carry a weapon or climb a rope? Is there a hat in the business that does not appear in the rendering? Has the director given you business with your costume that will affect its construction? I caused Leonato to appear in shirtsleeves in *Much Ado About Nothing* and to put his doublet on while on stage. That meant the designer had to alter the actor's shirt, line the doublet, and make the buttons practical. Has the director changed actions or text in such a fashion that you will have a fast change where you might not otherwise have had one—and might that require the designer to adjust the way the costume works? Is there something about the way *you* are developing the character which you hope the costume might present? In short, tell the designer anything that has developed since the designs were approved.

He can help you by explaining how certain garments ought properly to be worn (most applicable in period plays), what stances or actions will show you off to advantage, how the colors and textures of your costume relate you to other characters in the play, and how you can manage such difficult actions as a deep curtsy or a wrestling match in the garments you'll be wearing. If he doesn't volunteer such advice, ask questions. Parade about in your costume to get the feel of it. Try out some of the things you'll have to do in it, so you won't be surprised later. The costume designer is one of the few people working on the show that you are expected to question directly, without the stage manager as an intermediary. Perhaps this behavior results from his particular expertise, or perhaps it results from the fact that your initial encounters with him occur outside rehearsals, in the wardrobe shop or some rental company's dressing room. No one else is about, so it makes sense for you to discuss your common problems. This will hold true throughout the rehearsal period. Even in final dress rehearsals, when you may be receiving your costume notes through the director, it is correct behavior for you to ask specific questions of the costume designer or his assistants.

The costumers, cutters, and tailors are those craftsmen who actually build the costumes or rebuild old costumes to suit the present needs. These are among the unsung heroes of most productions and merit your politest behavior. For inexplicable reasons, most costume departments are placed in rooms without natural light or sufficient ventilation. Usually they are deep underground. Also, all costume departments are under-equipped, under-staffed, and given too small a space in which to work. Result? Bleary-eyed moles with bleeding fingers who are justified in feeling martyred, neglected, and generally malcontented. You are their pipeline to the outside world, just as they are your lifeline to a good costume. You can help each other.

Visit the costume shop, even when you are not called. (This pertains only if the costume shop is a part of your company. If costumes are rented, or if the shop is far from the rehearsal hall, forget this.) Your goal is to keep them abreast of the show's development, to help build their morale. Consider this as a social call which will have pleasant repercussions—special care will be taken with your costume, or yours will be available for use earlier than others'. In these visits, always be supportive and constructive. Don't engage in divisive gossip. Because they are isolated from rehearsals, costumers frequently become the gossip centers in a theatre. As they grow increasingly tired, the gossip grows proportionately vicious. Don't contribute. Bring good reports of the show's development.

Your major contact with the costumers will come at fittings. Here, as earlier with the designer, ask questions and relay information. Since your last visit has the director introduced the idea of blood bags for your death scene? Has the stage manager gotten this information to the costume department? Have you introduced a handkerchief into a scene which requires a pocket to be built onto your dressing robe? Additionally, there are some common courtesies you should observe in all fittings. Be prompt. Actors are notoriously naughty about being on time for fittings. Since the costume department is even more pressured than you are, you must respect their problems and get to your call promptly. Don't rush the fitters. Never mind that you want to leave shortly. Their work takes time, is exacting, and serves you. Plan to spend relaxed time at your fittings. Take care to be clean when you come to a fitting. Costumers have to work with and around your body. Make it presentable. Wash. Make certain your breath is inoffensive. Be certain to have on clean clothes, particularly clean underclothes: socks, bras, etc. Make certain you bring with you any support garments which might be necessary to the proper fitting of your costume. Women, bring your long-line bra with you so your costume can be properly fitted. Men, bring your dance belts if you'll be wearing tights. It is essential that you handle your costumes carefully. Hang things up after you've tried them on. Keep all your costumes and accessories tidily together, so no time is lost in looking for stray belts and shawls. Finally, thank the people who've helped you. When you leave they're going to work on your costume; a courteous "thank you" is never amiss.

At the dress parade you first encounter the production's wardrobe crew, the dressers and menders who will assist you through all costume rehearsals and performances. You will have daily commerce with this crew, and you will get service in direct ratio to your courteous behavior. If you're polite and treat them as the co-workers they truly are, you'll find your shoes shined regularly and your dresser in place for your quick change. These workers take pride in their contribution to the show and do not like being treated as second-class citizens. If you bark at them you may expect them to lose interest in helping you, and suddenly you'll find yourself desperately trying to make that quick change all alone.

At the dress parade, follow instructions. Typically, you'll be told to put on one costume, come to the wings, take your turn on the stage, then return it to your dressing room and follow the same procedure with all your other costumes. Don't waste time in this tedious but all-important exercise. You will do a lot of waiting around, but don't you be the cause of anyone else's waiting. You may feel excited to be in your finished costume for the first time, seeing other characters in theirs, but don't rush about showing yours off to your friends. The goal of a dress parade is to make a nearly final check of all costumes. The director and costume designer are out front taking notes and nobody needs you to preen about wasting time. You can contribute to a quick and valuable dress parade by being quiet! Your excitement will tempt you to gabble. Resist the temptation. There are people working who don't need their concentrations muddled by your small-talk. And finally, don't panic. True, your pants aren't ready and you look silly in your doublet and levis, but it is precisely to create a list of work to be completed that this parade is being held. Don't rain on it.

When your turn comes to go on the stage, do so quickly and simply. You'll be given instructions like "turn around," "put your hands over your head," and "wear the cape in Act Two." Typically, you'll be asked for any notes you have. Report any incompletions: no shoelaces, no cufflinks. Report problems: "I really can't sit down without splitting the breeches," and then demonstrate the problem. Ask questions: "How should the hat be worn?" "What jewelry should I wear?" "Which scenes do I use the raincoat in?" If there is a lull in the session, as director and costume designer confer out front, move about in the costume to demonstrate for them how it hangs and moves. When you are told "Thank you, next," leave the stage and make room for your successor.

Return all parts of your costume to their proper places. Hang up all costume pieces that should be on hangers. A sure sign of an amateur is a costume piled thoughtlessly on a chair. Make certain that all accessories are carefully stored: hats, swords, boots, collar pins, barrettes, etc. Your job, not to mention your performance, requires you to attend to your costume.

Observe all rules for the care of costumes. It is common for actors to be told they may not eat or drink or smoke in costume. The younger the company, the more these policies will be stressed. The producer doesn't have the money to pay for a new costume after you spill catsup all over yourself, and the costumers don't have the time to build you another. A sensible way to accommodate any such rules and your own habits is to bring a dressing smock with you, to wear over your costume when you want to eat or smoke.

Take good care of your costume. Report any problems to maintenance quickly. Usually there is a sheet of paper and a pencil posted on the callboard for just such notes. Shine your shoes, if your character would have well-shined shoes. The audience sees your feet and measures you, in part, by their appearance. Management is required to have your costumes laundered and dry cleaned once a week. That usually happens on the day off, say Monday. That means things are getting wilted towards the weekend, when your largest and highest paying audience sees the show. Care enough about your work to give them their money's worth. Put on your makeup *before* your costume, so you don't get liner, rouge, and powder all over it. If you have to touch up your makeup during a performance, cover yourself with a towel or smock. In short, deal with your costume as carefully as you do all parts of your performance.

CREWS   Suddenly there are lots of people working the show. You have moved into the theatre and while for four weeks the show was only an intense band of actors, now there are electricians, stagehands, flymen, prop men, and an entire army of skilled, efficient workers. They don't know you and aren't in awe of you. Worse, unlike a school circumstance where all such jobs are filled by frightened seventeen-year-olds, these workers are forty-five and smoke pipes. How do you adjust to this? How do you behave towards them?

Sadly, the typical young actor assumes a nose-in-the-air attitude. "After all," he feels, "I am young, talented, beautiful, and the artist without whom this show cannot go on." If those thoughts go through your mind and influence your attitude towards the crews, you're in for a bad time. For a moment, think what they're thinking. "Who is this punk? I've worked this theatre for twenty-five years. I've worked with the greats like Gielgud, Logan, and Fonda. I know more about theatre in my broken little finger than he'll know in ten years—if he's still in the business, which I doubt." The experienced stagehand is a part of the theatre family, an old and proven member. You are the new boy on the block. The distinction between crew and cast is mostly in the egotistical mind of the performer. From the management's point of view, both are important workers. They need to get along together.

Two guidelines to your behavior with the crews: respect their work and be courteous. The same rules apply throughout your theatre work. The crews know their jobs. Unlike the seventeen-year-old prop mistress who rattles easily and is doing her job under protest because she really wants to be an actress, a professional prop master knows his job, does it without flap, and enjoys doing it well. He also gets paid handsomely for it. (He'll work many more weeks a year than you will and no doubt will earn substantially more. In a commercial world in which your value is in part measured by your ability to earn, he has much better credentials than you have, so forget the notion that you are more important because you're an actor.) Unless you are playing a leading role, and as a beginner that's not likely, you'll spend a lot of hours backstage. If you make friends with the crews you'll enjoy a sip of coffee, an occasional cigarette, and some pleasant small talk. Your time will pass pleasantly, if you're a member of the family.

PRODUCERS   You might be cast in a show, rehearse it, perform it for 35 weeks, close it, go on a 20-week national tour, return to New York, and never once speak to your producer. You will have seen him a few times, but you may never have been introduced. He is the businessman who sits on top of the economic, political, and artistic pyramids. You are near the base of that pyramid, as the flow chart earlier revealed. You are one of the building blocks with which the producer has made the event happen.

There are many types of producers, but all have one thing in common—they are businessmen. There are tough lawyers, like David Merrick. There are show-biz radicals, like Joe Papp, and former whiz-kids like Harold Prince. There are bright young men and failed actors and sick old accountants and nearly every breed of human.

The producer is responsible for everything. He raises the money to do the show, chooses the show, hires everyone who will work on it, works to improve the script, the performances, the advance sales, and the company's morale. He lives in a continual world of crises: the set won't be ready on time, the critics won't come because of a conflict and the opening has to be shifted, the star has a cold, the theatre parties aren't selling, and the director needs to work the company overtime and that means money, and there isn't any more in the budget! By comparison, your complaints that the dressing rooms are dirty and the box office treasurer rude seem rather petty. Small wonder the producer is remote from you; your responsibilities are on very different planes.

There are three times you're likely to meet the producer. You may encounter him during casting—as you sign your contract, at the first rehearsal, or perhaps during your audition. At such a meeting, he is the boss and you the job applicant. He is a capitalist and will exploit you if he possibly can. Also, he is a lover, in love with the forthcoming production, and he wants to make you happy and welcome. So he will be all smiles as he offers you less money than you were hoping he would. But you also are a lover, hoping the next weeks will stretch into months and that the affair will be a wonderful one, so you smile too, as you compromise yourself. After all, a happy job at minimum is better than no job at all. If you are wise you will have learned the producer's name before you meet him. But your encounter will normally be limited to a handshake and a three-sentence exchange of banalities.

You will next encounter the producer when he shows up at a rehearsal. And he will, whether he is producing a $1,200,000 Broadway musical or an experimental production in a university drama department. In a L.O.R.T. company he is the Managing Director or Chairman of the Board. In a stock company he is the Producing Director. At a university he is the Chairman of the Department. Whoever he is, and no matter how inobtrusively he enters, he sends everyone into a panic. The higher up the pyramid you are, the more nervous you will be when the boss starts looking over your shoulder. The director and the star will be the most nervous, as they have the greatest responsibility for the way things are going. As a supporting player you will feel relatively unthreatened, and yet in the back of your mind you'll know that if he hates what you're doing, he may talk with the director about replacing you. So now you're panicked. What to do? Pretend it is a performance. Everyone will say "it's only a rehearsal, just go about your business as usual," but no one will believe that. You're not ready for a public performance, but give one anyway. Turn on your performance concentration, your public calm, and act the hell out of your scenes. By doing so you'll achieve several ends. You'll make it possible for yourself to get through the day. You'll show the producer what he came to see, a preview of coming attractions. And you'll help settle down the actors who share scenes with you. You may not actually talk to the boss during this encounter but your behavior can have an important influence on your working relationship with him.

Lastly, you will meet the producer at social gatherings. These may be at the beginning of rehearsals, just prior to a tryout tour, informally following an out-of-town opening, or at the inevitable opening night party—whether that happens on a darkened stage with communion wine from the cathedral next door as the beverage or at Sardi's. At any social gathering the producer is both host and star. Around him, in concentric circles, are the backers (or board if it's an institutional theatre), the director and the stars, professional and personal friends, his staff, and lastly the actors. If he enjoys mingling among the masses, you may exchange a greeting or two and shake his hand. During such gatherings it is wise to remember that the producer believes he has created you. You're his toy, and he may introduce you to his acquaintances or to members of the press as though you were his private possession. He's a 17th-century benevolent despot and patron of the arts who keeps you about because he believes in culture. You can resist this relationship if you wish to endanger your chances of working for him again, but you'd be wisest to tug at your forelock and smile at his patronage.

PUBLIC RELATIONS   You are part of a business. You are a commodity to be marketed, both as yourself and as a component of a show that must be sold to a resisting public. When you deal with your show's PR department (or with your agent), you must temporarily put aside all notions of yourself as an "artist" and recognize that the same devices that lead you to buy one brand of soup instead of another are the ones that will guide some ticket buyer to come to your show instead of the one across the street. We live in an advertiser's world and we succeed to the extent that we realize this truth and do our PR work well. Accordingly, as an actor, you must cooperate fully with the professional PR people who've been engaged to promote you.

At the same time, you need not totally sell out your own sense of taste and dignity. If the PR department wants to put your nude picture on the poster to be distributed about town, and you think that is not in the best interests of your career, say "No." You have the right of approval on most ads and releases, and certainly on program copy, and you may use your own best judgment in these matters.

Recognize that PR people are professionals who deal in the business world regularly. They respond to promptness, courtesy, and clarity. If you've been scheduled to meet with the guy knocking out a new release about you, be on time. He has a deadline that can't wait upon your whimsy. Come prepared. Bring with you some photos (more than one pose, if possible), some copies of your resumé, and anything that might give him a particular angle for the story: have you broken your leg during rehearsals? Did you get cast because you were the only one-legged Lithuanian to audition?

Volunteer for any promotional activities you can. Exposure is a valuable aid to your career and if you can get an interview in the paper or if you appear in a TV spot, you'll do yourself and your show a world of good. Be generous with your time.

Write your own bio for the program. No one will ask you to, but if you write your own (and if it is reasonable) you can insist it be used. If you write it, you'll be certain it says what you wish it to say and in the tone you wish to use in advancing yourself to your public, and to other possible future employers. If you're joining a permanent company, check past programs to learn the length and tone of bios. If yours is a commercial production, inquire of the PR head what kind of bios will be needed. As a rule, I bring mine with me to the first rehearsal for a show. At that time I know I'll be asked to fill out a brief form for the PR department. I simply attach my bio to that form.

Photography is a major part of public relations work and you will be photographed many times for each job. Some photos may be taken during rehearsals, to be used for press releases or in souvenir programs. Over the years you will grow accustomed to photographers moving about you, clicking away as you work. The stage manager and/or director will normally protect you from over-zealous and intrusive cameramen, particularly those prone to use flashbulbs. But if your work is really being disrupted by a photographer a brief word to the stage manager will set things right. Modern lenses and film speeds permit photographers to work in poor light, so photographers may roam in front of the stage (and in the wings) during run-throughs and final dresses. Your task is to go about your business. Pretend you're in a performance and the clicking sound is some unidentifiable audience noise which you will not allow to disturb your concentration.

Photo calls are another matter. These are special sessions dedicated entirely to the photographer. They may occur on the stage, at his studio, on location in some park, or anywhere the photographer and producer agree upon. A photo call is a part of your working day. Equity stipulates the amount of time permitted for a photo call and it is reasonable. Particularly if you remember that the primary use for all photos is to promote your show. A standard photo call happens during the final week of rehearsals and follows a dress run-through. You'll be tired, anxious to get your notes and a shower, but you'll have to hang around while some outsider snaps photos. If your stage manager is top flight, the session will be well-organized and progress smoothly. A list of the photos to be taken (the points in the action will be identified by lines of dialogue) should be posted so you'll know in advance which shots you're in and how many costume changes you need to make—and in what order. Good behavior on your part will get you through this session gracefully. Don't waste time. If you have a costume change to make, complete it by the time your next photo is called. Don't wander off and make someone come searching for you. Keep quiet. There is an immense temptation to release your tensions through wisecracks. Resist the temptation. Deal with the photo call as an important segment of your working day. Respect the photographer and his problems. Who knows, the picture he snaps may end up in front of the theatre, attract the attention of an underground film maker as he strolls by, and lead you to stardom. Or it may be a delightful souvenir to send to your mother.

COMPANY MANAGER AND GENERAL MANAGER   These two people are part of the producer's administrative team. Sometimes one person does both jobs, but in a large company the duties are split. The general manager is the business administrator for the production and handles most money and logistical matters. The company manager is his link to the actors. Normally, the company manager will come to rehearsals once a week to bring you your pay and to get you to sign for it. Your pay may come in check form or in cash, depending on your agreement (your deputy will represent you) with the producer. The company manager will also assist you with job-related problems such as how to find accommodations if you're away from your place of residence, what banks will honor your checks, what doctors, hospitals, and dentists you should contact in case of emergency, how to file for Workman's Compensation in the event of accident, and a myriad of other problems that arise. He is engaged to assist you. He will be your contact for tickets if friends or agents wish to see the show. (You will have to pay for these, of course. You are paid your salary because seats are sold. But he'll be able to get you seats, even if the house is nominally sold out.) He'll help you get seats to other events in town if you're traveling. He'll arrange your transportation from one city to the next. He'll arrange your hotel accommodations while you're on tour. He'll attend to many of your needs. I don't think I need to point out how important it is for you to be on his good side.

FRONT OF HOUSE   You're not likely to have much traffic with the house manager, box office treasurer, or other front-of-house personnel, but it behooves you to remember that they are the permanent cadre in the theatre and that you are the transient guest. When your show closes, they'll be working on the next show which rents the space. (This is even true to a degree in institutional and educational theatres since their staffs also present film series, lecture series, and concerts.) You will get along with the front-of-house staff if you extend to them the same respect and courtesy you show elsewhere. Then, if you need the house manager to take special care in showing your aged aunt to her seat, you can count on his showing you appropriate respect and courtesy.

YOURSELF   The theatre is a public arena in which creativity and business co-exist through the cooperative workings of many people. You will prosper in this arena if you understand its workings, the relationships between people that formulate its political structure, and the obligation each has to respect his fellows and to pull his own weight. And that means, finally, that each must respect himself. You will gain self-respect through attention to your craft, experience, and love of the art which you create. As Stanislavsky taught us many years ago, "Love the art in yourself, not yourself in the art."

Preparing for Rehearsals

"I couldn't find it," you say as you pant into the first rehearsal eight minutes late. Some beginning! Actors are looking at you through weary eyes, the stage manager is silently rehearsing his reprimand, the director has lost the edge he had for his opening remarks and is disgruntled, and the company manager is thinking about the five-day clause. It may take you a week of hard work to earn back the company's confidence—all because you didn't prepare properly for rehearsals.

The first thing to do, if there is ample time between learning of your casting and reporting for your first day's work, is to put all your "civilian" duties in order. Pay the bills, write your correspondence, negotiate your leave of absence with your employer, cancel any unnecessary medical or social appointments, get your bank account balanced, your clothes laundered, your apartment cleaned, and your grocery shopping done. You're about to enter into a three-week period in which you simply won't have time for the daily exercises of living. In addition to all the preparations you may need to do to play the role (research the writer or the period, learn the lines, analyze the script, secure a dialect coach, etc.) you must make appropriate preparations to go to work.

Next, make certain that your rehearsal kit is in order. As it may be the same as your audition kit there may not be a great deal to do, but check it all the same. You may not need as extensive a supply of medical aides, as the stage manager will supply most of your wants, but check to insure you have breath mints and aspirin. Make sure your calendar book is up to date, so you can enter all photo calls, costume calls, and special rehearsals into it. Put in a supply of pencils, paper, and the like. Prepare your rehearsal clothes. Are you going to need a rehearsal skirt? A double-breasted suit coat? Three-inch heels? A fedora? And what kind of shoes will you want to rehearse in? What PR materials will you need? Photo? A bio from your previous show? A new bio? Well, whatever you can imagine you'll need, get it ready. A rehearsal period is a bit like a trip. You have to pack carefully if you're going to be comfortable on your way.

Scout the terrain. Discover where the rehearsal hall is and how you can get there. Check the comparative rates of parking lots. Investigate the traveling time needed by car, bus, or subway. Decide on your best route before you find yourself eight minutes late. Then check the neighborhood. Are there parts of it that seem unsafe? If so, are there preferred routes to the rehearsal hall and preferred times of day to travel on particular routes? (For example, it is fine to go to the theatre by subway in the daytime but safer to take the bus home if the rehearsal goes past 6:30 PM.) Investigate the neighborhood for drugstores, restaurants, and bars. Compare prices, so you don't spend your first week's paycheck on lunches alone. At first, any new neighborhood seems forbidding and alien. But you're going to be working in this one for several weeks, and your work requires you to be relaxed, so you'll help yourself by familiarizing yourself with your new haunts before you set to work.

If the terrain is in a new town, your task is a bit more elaborate. You have to find accommodations, learn the transport system, and set up housekeeping. (This is true for stock or resident theatre engagements mostly. Problems you'll encounter touring will be discussed later.) Generally, the company manager will be your guide through all this. Many stock and resident companies have duplicated information sheets which provide you with the names of reputable doctors, boarding houses, merchants, and restaurants. These frequently list shops that will give discounts to actors and places you must stay away from. At the Utah Shakespearean Festival we used to provide arriving actors with a list of bars to avoid. These were frequented by cowboys who were suspicious of strangers, particularly those with long hair and eastern accents, and who loved to have three beers and then go out "to get 'em a Shakespeare." If you are heading for a new town, allow yourself ample time. Don't try to drive in the morning of the first rehearsal and hope to go to work and get settled simultaneously. It can be done—indeed it's done all too often—but your work will suffer if you try it. Those first three days of rehearsal are tough and they merit and require your 100% attention.

The Daily Work Pattern

The alarm clock rings. You do your morning ablutions, eat a healthy breakfast, and then get ready for the day's work.

Set the day's work in focus. What is going to be done that day? Check the rehearsal schedule and recollect what the director said at the end of yesterday's rehearsal. Know what segment of the play is going to be worked on and go over it carefully in your head. Then set yourself a goal for the day. "Today I shall fall in love with Othello." This essential aspect of your role hasn't been achieved yet, and without it many of your actions, lines, and emotions are forced, unbelievable. By setting a task for yourself you bring your work into focus. You will do many other things as well—some will come from the direction you'll receive and others will evolve spontaneously as you work—but with a specific task in mind, you'll be assured of progress during the day's work.

Now do your warm-ups. These may be physical warm-ups for your voice and body or they may be warm-ups for the techniques of your internal process. Will you use emotional recall to help you fall in love with Othello? Then warm up your concentration. If your task for the day is to find your character's physical carriage, and you hope to do it through observation, get out and observe people. Use your tools as a way of warming up for the rehearsal and apply them to the specific goal you've set for yourself.

Lastly, make certain you have everything you need to take with you, and go.

Your arrival at the rehearsal hall should be early, quiet, and cordial. Get to the hall early enough to complete your warm-ups so that you're ready to work when the stage manager calls "Places, please." Greet your comrades but be alert to the fact that others may already be working, so don't burst into the room. Actors may have decided to arrive early to work together on a scene; the designer and stage manager may be deep in consultation; the writer may be urging changes on the director. The world doesn't necessarily begin with your entrance. Of course, if no one is doing anything special, you can make all the noise you need to.

Every time you come into the rehearsal hall you should check
for notices. If there's a callboard, check it for information about
costume fittings, PR interviews, changes in the rehearsal schedule, and anything else that might pertain to you. If there's no
board, ask the stage manager if there's anything you need to
know. (If you're working in a film, check the shooting schedule
on your arrival. It tells the sequence in which the day's shots will
be taken; there are commonly changes from 6:00 p.m. one night to
8:00 a.m. the following day.)

Now you're ready to rehearse. The director determines what is
to be rehearsed and how the rehearsal is to be conducted. There
are many standard kinds of rehearsal, each of which has its own
procedures and goals. These include:

Meetings   These usually deal with business details
such as the election of an equity deputy or discussion
of transportation to another city or theatre. The goal is
dissemination of information.

Readings   The script is read out loud and discussed.
Commonly each actor reads his own role, but sometimes
the playwright or director will read the entire script as
a way of communicating his feelings about it. I know of
one instance in which actors read any role but their
own—I never understood the intention. The goal of
readings is to experience the entirety of the play and to
begin to hear it as it will be spoken by the voices
assigned to each role.

Discussions   These are always led by the director,
though the playwright, designers, and choreographer
may be asked to contribute. Primarily these are rehearsals in which the director and actor explore the nature
of characters, intentions of scenes, motivations for
actions, and tonality of sequences. The device of discussion is a rational one, and logic and rhetoric are the
obvious tools. The goal is to achieve increased understanding of the play.

Games   These rehearsals are commonly based on the
exercises developed by Viola Spolin. The actors, under
the director's guidance, play various childlike games,
some of which may relate to the basic action of the play
or to one of its scenes. The goals of games are many: to
create a relaxed atmosphere in which to work, to kindle

the creative spirit, to establish mutual trust, to encounter the play on non-rational terms.

Improvisations   Like games, improvisations are paratheatrical. Actors, always under tutelage, act out situations which relate to or extend from the characters they
are playing and the situations those characters are in.
For example, the character has a fight with her brother
before entering into a scene. That fight could be improvised between the actors. Or, the action of the play is
the healing of a society's political wounds; the director
could create an improvisation which gives his actors an
analogous experience. The goal of improvisation is to
flesh out the actor's sense of his character's experience.

Staging or blocking   Rehearsals in which the rough
outline of the actors' movements are determined. Sometimes this is achieved improvisationally, using games
and improvs. More commonly the director instructs the
actors where to go and when. The goals are to achieve a
beginning physicalization of the play and concurrently
to express each character's actions in spatial terms.

Working rehearsals   Rehearsals in which the director
and actor work towards a rich, complete, and polished
expression of some segment of the play. These rehearsals are the "meat" of a rehearsal period, and commonly
employ all the techniques at the director's disposal. Discussion and improvisation fuse. Blocking is improvised
and readings recur. The distinguishing trait of working
rehearsals is repetition, as each word, thought, and
move is repeated in an attempt to "get it right." The
goal is to move slowly towards a deeply felt and
externally controlled performance.

Special Rehearsals   These are rehearsals in which
some particular problem is confronted, and they are
frequently supervised by one of the director's assistants.
Dance and music rehearsals are obvious examples. But
rehearsals of nude scenes, scenes of violence, and private coaching sessions are also included. The techniques employed relate to the kind of special rehearsal,
though show-and-tell is commonly used. The goal is to
select a special task in the production and to refine it
towards performance.

Run-throughs   Rehearsals in which the actors proceed
through all or a stipulated portion of the play without

interruption. Typically, the director sits out front and takes notes which he later gives to the actors. The goals of a run-through are to provide everyone with a sense of what has been accomplished to that point in the rehearsal process, to identify areas of the play requiring intensive work, and to give the actors a sense of continuity in their performances.

Technical rehearsals. Rehearsals in which the scenery, lighting, properties, and sound elements of production are given total focus. Commonly, a "cue-to-cue" rehearsal is conducted by the stage manager in which the actors are told on what line to pick up the action and then are told to stop when the cue has been executed. Commonly this rehearsal requires extensive repetition. The goal is to integrate production elements into the action.

Dress rehearsals Rehearsals in which costumes are worn, usually for the first time. Commonly a dress parade will precede a run-through in costume, the two events comprising the first dress rehearsal. The goal is to introduce this element of production into the action.

Previews Rehearsals of the entire show under performance circumstances, with an audience in attendance. The goal is to discover the audience's responses, so that subsequent working rehearsals (usually held the following afternoon) can make adjustments in script or action which will lead to an increasingly favorable response.

Brush-up rehearsals Rehearsals called after a production has formally opened and usually conducted by the production stage manager. The goals of these rehearsals are to refresh the actors' performances after a hiatus, or to restore to the original execution sequences which have altered undesirably during a long run.

Understudy rehearsals Rehearsals conducted by the P.S.M. to prepare understudies should they have to perform. Understudies are always required to duplicate the performance they are "covering" in movement, interpretation, tempo, and execution to the best of their abilities.

At the end of the day's rehearsal, gather your things together and check for final notices. Read the callboard or check with the stage manager, but make certain you know everything you need to know about tomorrow's work.

You may want to do some socializing with your fellow actors as a way of unwinding; do so. It is very useful to know your colleagues on a private level. All work and no play makes you a dull actor. Two beers at a neighborhood pub is an important part of your working day.

But you have work yet to do, so take it easy. After dinner, plan to spend two or three hours doing your homework. (I'll discuss the kinds of homework you might do shortly.) Before you undertake it, though, reflect on the goal you had set yourself for the day. Did you accomplish it? Did you "fall in love with Othello?" If you accomplished your goal, great. If you didn't, you have nonetheless had a focus to your day's work, and you'll have other days to confront that problem again. It's a poor notion to wrestle with the same problem two days in succession, as it's easy to develop a block—and that's counter-productive.

Now do your homework.

And now . . . relax. It may be hard for you to let go after an intensive day, but you need to. You need to chat with friends, watch television, play a game or otherwise get your mind and body away from your work. A thirteen-hour work day is enough! So for a brief time leave the actor in you behind and return to being the pleasant and social creature you really are. It will make the people who live with you a bit more tolerant and it will help you to return to the next day's work refreshed.

And now to sleep. Allow yourself plenty of time for rest. You'll be no good to yourself or anyone else if you work half the night and arrive at rehearsal bleary-eyed. Get a full night's sleep— that's part of your daily work pattern too.

And be certain to set your alarm.

Dismissal, Replacement, and Understudying

"You're fired!" There are elaborate ways of saying it, but when you get down to the truth of it, those are the words that say it clearest. When it happens, it will be the hardest moment in your life as an actor. The rejection you have courted and feared is given concrete reality. You can rationalize why you weren't cast in a show, or why you weren't given the role you preferred, but being fired is being fired. It's a blow to your ego, your craft, and your pocketbook.

There are many reasons why you might be dismissed. Perhaps you've not learned the lessons of this handbook and your professional attitude is poor. You're tardy, lazy, or, like the young man described on the opening page of this book, you're an argumentative nuisance. Or perhaps someone in the production has enough "muscle" to get you dismissed because he doesn't like working with you or because he's got a friend he'd rather have playing the role. You could be the victim of politics. But most often, when you're fired, it's because the director or the producer wants somebody better. Ouch! You're fired because you're not good enough!

"It isn't fair," you howl. Well, whoever said the theatre was fair? If your training and experience have been in a school, you may have the false impression that rehearsals are for the purpose of your improvement and that if the director would only work with you, you'd *be* good enough. But rehearsals are for the purpose of teaching actors who *are* good enough the particular tasks of this production. You were fired because you couldn't cut it.

When it happens, brevity is the best policy. Don't protest, don't cause a scene, don't try to discuss the situation, don't plead, and don't haggle. Pick up your possessions, find out how you'll get your final check, and go. Any other behavior will cause you extended embarrassment and grief, will embarrass your fellow actors (rupturing your friendships with them), and will disrupt rehearsals. You won't change your fate, and you'll do damage to the production. You must love the theatre more than you love yourself. That's hard to remember when you've just lost your only paycheck, but the show is going to go on without you, so let it.

Recently, I was party to a particularly ugly firing. Most of the ugliness resulted from people's misguided attempts to behave in a kindly manner. A five-person play had been rehearsed and was in performance. The producer had seen a rehearsal and discussed with his young director his view that the juvenile couldn't cut it. The director assured the producer he'd work with the boy and that a satisfactory performance would result. The producer wanted to be kindly, so he acquiesced. The show went into previews and the backers saw it. They told the producer the juvenile was bad. He relayed this to the director and a replacement was secretly engaged and rehearsed. When the replacement was ready, the producer told the stage manager to fire the original boy and put the replacement into the show. The young director asked to share the odious task with the stage manager. He wanted to ease the dismissal for the actor by providing him with an explanation, but of course he only made things uglier. The actor complained, insulted, pleaded, and had an awful time accepting his dismissal. Later he called the other actors, asking for their sympathy, and ended in making them afraid they might be next in some purge. Finally the actor called the producer who told him very directly that he had hired the actor against his own better judgment, refrained from firing him earlier as a courtesy to the director, but had now given order for the dismissal. End of discussion. The producer can hire and the producer can fire. And as an actor, you have little recourse except what your contract stipulates—severance pay. And there is nothing to discuss, no argument to be made. You're fired because the boss wants to hire somebody else.

How can you help yourself after you've been fired? First, calmly, discern why you were fired. If you can honestly conclude you were the victim of politics, or if you were canned because you couldn't sing well enough and the error was the director's for casting you, your ego need not be too bruised. If you were released because you were deficient in some skill, set about improving your skills: take classes, work to broaden your employability. But if you conclude you were canned because you weren't good enough, you have some hard thinking to do. Are you in the right business? Can you cut it as an actor? If you're not a mountain climber, all the desire in the world won't get you to the top of Mt. Everest. You must have skills, stamina, courage, and a talent for climbing. As an actor you must have desire, but desire alone won't get you employment. Any time you're fired is the time to reflect on your chosen career and to consider other ways of spending your life.

☆ ☆ ☆ ☆ ☆

You may be engaged to understudy or to replace. As a beginner it is likely you'll be hired to play a small role and also to "cover" one or more larger roles. As an understudy, your individual creativity is not welcome. You're engaged to duplicate what someone else has done and you're a good employee to the extent that your performance repeats his. Understudying is a frustrating business.

It is an actor's fantasy that the star will fall sick and you'll go on and become a star. Judy Garland sang the fantasy in *A Star Is Born* and the real thing happened when Judy Holliday went into the leading role of *Born Yesterday* in Philadelphia. But it won't happen to you. Instead, you'll be under-rehearsed and ill-prepared. You'll get notice at half-hour that you're going on and for thirty minutes you'll panic, trying to remember the words and fit into a strange costume. You'll bumble through the show, perhaps even playing it for a few performances. At each performance, your name will be announced to the audience and they'll groan, correctly assuming you're an under-rehearsed and ill-prepared second choice. Finally, the principal will recover, start playing the role again, and you'll be back where you were, saying, "Dinner is served."

If you are understudying you must try to be inobtrusive. Some actors are made uneasy by the knowledge that someone is ready to take over for them. Never mind that Equity requires them to be understudied. Never mind that everyone in the show is being understudied. Some actors are so insecure that your presence at rehearsals rattles them. You can help in two ways. First, don't try to help by discussing the problem. Don't walk up to the actor and attempt to denigrate what you're doing; he'll never believe you and will grow even more nervous. Just leave him to wrestle with his paranoia on his own. (If he's unthreatened and wants to help you, he'll approach you. Then you can open up.) Secondly, give the false impression that you're not taking your work very seriously. Let the actor believe you're slacking and couldn't really do the role, even in an emergency. Then he'll regain his confidence, because he'll realize how much the show depends on him.

Equity stipulates that all understudies must be ready to go on. Understudies rarely are. After a production has opened there are only two understudy rehearsals a week, not nearly enough to learn a role. During the rehearsal period for the show there are never understudy rehearsals. That means you're on your own. When the show opens, you must be ready to step into the role. And you've never been rehearsed in it. Madness? Absolutely. Your only recourse is to watch carefully at rehearsals, use the stage manager's prompt script as often as you can get at it, and work a lot on your own.

If you're engaged to replace, you have a bit more flexibility in creating the role than you have as an understudy. If you're replacing during the rehearsal period, you have to pick up the blocking as it's already established, and certain general attacks on interpretation, character relationships, and rhythms, but you'll be able to rework everything during the remaining rehearsals and the performance can be largely your own. The only limitation in this circumstance is time. You've got to work faster than you might like to.

If you're replacing an actor who's leaving, you may get a reasonable amount of rehearsal time. You'll be obliged to repeat the basic interpretation of the departing actor, his blocking, execution of specific business, and anything that seriously affects other performers. But during your rehearsals, and during your early performances, you'll commonly be given a bit of leeway so you can make the performance your own. I watched Leonard Frey prepare the title role in Moliere's *The Imaginary Invalid* in one week. He was replacing E.G. Marshall, who had another commitment. Frey worked each morning on his lines. He had a five-hour rehearsal each afternoon with two understudies who helped him through various sequences. (The stage manager was conducting the rehearsals, of course.) And he watched every performance of the show. He then had two run-throughs with the full cast, and he was ready. It was a pretty dazzling display. His performance was very different from Marshall's though his basic business made no changes that would disturb the rest of the cast. Our jobs were to adjust to his performance, as his was the important one.

If you replace during the rehearsal period, you walk into a tense situation. Most of the company is anxious for you to do well, as they've been aware of the unsatisfactory work of your predecessor, but others may have been friends with the departed actor. You can help yourself and the company by observing common-sense rules of behavior. Don't talk about the other actor. Work as though you were starting from scratch. Get the basic blocking from the prompt script immediately, and learn it. Learn the script as fast as you can. By getting these mechanics out of the way you'll be able to rehearse the scenes, and you'll assure the rest of the company that they can rely on you. Be extremely flexible in developing exchanges with the other actors—try to supply them with the line readings and business they request.

Once you've caught up with the others and are rehearsing as an equal member of the company, you can assert yourself and work as you would normally. But it is useful to remember that you've been engaged as a medicated bandage. You can't contribute to the show's organic development until you've healed the sore.

Homework

What can you do to help yourself? What can you do between the time you leave rehearsal one day and return to rehearsal the following day? Sadly, many actors can do very little. Oh yes, they can learn their lines and think through some specific business, but most are overly dependent on their directors and if that's true for you, you're not ready to accept employment. A director wants you to come to each rehearsal with something new. He wants you to work on your own. To do so, you need both a method of working and sufficient discipline to make yourself use it. There are two types of work you can do between rehearsals: work on the role and work on yourself. These are your homework.

Your work on your role must begin with an analysis of the script, and of your role in particular. Analysis is a rational process, a programmed and sequential investigation which uses established tools and methodology to achieve information and knowledge. You need a method to answer such questions as: What is the play about? What is the story? What does it mean? What does my character want? What is the character doing in the play in the first place? What theatrical style is the text and what relationship has that to my job? What are my relationships to the characters in the play? What are my actions, beats, transitions? And a thousand more. The Stanislavsky Method includes a system of analysis that most young actors have read about, but can't use. When the Actors Studio fell from fashion in the 1950's and when games and psycho-physical exercises became the core for most courses in actor training, the need for a rational method in creating a role was often forgotten. As a result, many actors have no method. Superficiality, inconsistency, and unfocused generalities mark too much of today's acting. This handbook on behavior is not the place to describe a method of analysis. It *is* a place to urge you to learn one. Without such a method all of your work is inferior and the best of work habits and professional manners will not make you a successful actor.

Let me assume you have analyzed your role. What should you do next? Study! Too many actors are intellectual lightweights. There's a great irony here, since so many of America's younger actors hold advanced academic degrees which allege they have a body of acquired information and a set of scholarly tools with which to learn more. All those MFA's ought to know their ways around the library. Do you? Do you know where to learn about the technique of Expressionist acting before you show up to rehearse *From Morn to Midnight?* Do you know where to learn about the daily customs of late 19th-century Russia before you begin rehearsing *The Sea Gull?* There are three types of research you ought to do on any play: research the author, the socio-historical setting of the play, and the psychological and physiological traits of your character. Let's consider each in turn.

You need to learn a great deal about the author. If he's not alive and well and working with you, you must rely on secondary sources and these are mostly in printed form. Begin by reading about his life. Biography is frequently helpful in understanding a playwright's attitudes towards people, human and social values, and even the specific subject matters that appear in his plays. Then read the playwright's other works. You will learn about his characters, the ideas he expresses, and the tonality of the play you're rehearsing by preparing in this manner. I was directing Neil Simon's *The Good Doctor* when I discovered the actress doing the short piece called "The Audition" had never read Chekhov's *The Three Sisters.* Since the character she was playing used a cutting of the three sisters' final speeches for her audition, it was imperative the actress read the play. She did so but only after I instructed her to. Her research was sorely deficient. Even for such seemingly self-contained work as Neil Simon's farces, research is essential.

You need to learn about the socio-historical setting of the play's action. How did people behave in the times? If you're in a Restoration comedy, it is not enough to know there was a "language of the fan"; you must learn sufficient details about it to select useful "vocabulary" from that language. If you're doing a contemporary play, you may be tempted to assume you know about the life and times and don't need to do any research.

Nonsense. What if you're asked to play the waitress in *When You Comin' Back, Red Ryder?* Have you ever worked as a waitress in a diner? Have you ever lived in the Southwest? There are many things about the world of the play which you need to know if you are to create your character fully. Some can only be learned in rehearsal, some can only be learned experientially, but some can be learned through research.

You need to know about the psychological and physiological traits of your character. If the script is written so that you can identify your character with contemporary psychological terminology, you might enrich your performance through a study of the type you're portraying. Is your character a youngest child? A sexually repressed introvert? A dangerous paranoiac? The tools of psychology help us to understand human behavior. Characters in plays are imitations of people. It can be useful to learn about people in order for you to learn about your character. The same applies for physical traits. An actor playing *Plaza Suite* for me researched the symptoms of glaucoma, as the first of the three characters in that show suffers from the disease. His findings about "tunnel vision" influenced both his physicalization of the role and his interpretation of the character who is suffering from an emotional tunnel vision as well.

Research is an unending process and you must use your common sense about it. As long as the research is contributing directly to your work, as long as it is not usurping your time and keeping you from essential or immediate requirements of your work, and as long as you can make specific use of your findings, keep it up. But when these three no longer obtain, it is time to leave the library, close the book, and get about your business.

If you share the widely held belief that acting is imitating human behavior, you can enrich your work by doing some observing. When directing a play about city policemen recently, I arranged for the actors to visit a police headquarters and to go on patrol one evening in squad cars. I wanted the actors to observe the real police officers' behavior. If your director doesn't arrange such an outing for you, make your own arrangements. Are you in a production of *Marat/Sade*? Do as the original cast did: go to an asylum. In short, imitate life, not someone else's imitation. Don't act the way you've seen an actor portray madness. Go to the primary source.

Perhaps the most important work you can do during the brief hours you have for your homework is to identify the key moments in each scene and prepare them. Given the limited time you'll have for homework, it is fair to assume you'll have to be selective in what you work on. Big emotional moments, entrances, and exits are most worthy of your energies, and in that order. You will commonly use emotional recall to develop your moments of profound emotion. The audience will believe your performance in proportion to its belief in your most exalted moments, so these merit a lot of time-consuming work. If you can achieve credibility in these moments during your homework, your work within the rehearsals will be truly productive—for your fellow actors as well as for yourself. If you are working on your entrances, work on the given circumstances so that you can arrive at the rehearsal the following day and enter the scene to be rehearsed with a full sense of the particular action. I was directing a show off-Broadway some years back and one scene called for a husband to arrive at his country home to find his emotionally unstable wife in the bedroom, and then to inquire why she had come, how long she had been there, and what she was doing. One rehearsal the actor entered, looked quietly about the room, walked to his wife's suitcases, lifted them, set them back down, and then went on with the scene. I was fascinated, but had no idea what he was doing or why it had seemed so compellingly right. At the end of the scene I asked about the business. "I was weighing them. I wanted to learn if she had unpacked yet," he explained. "Then I'd be able to guess if she was telling the truth when she answered me." It is just such particularized actions, devised outside rehearsals, which mark the fine actor, the actor who knows how to do his homework.

Your private homework also includes such mechanics as learning your lines and working out the timing of business. Profitable rehearsals depend on your knowing the mechanics of your job as early as you can. Forget all the self-delusions about line-learning as an organic or osmotic process; sit down early and learn the words. Until you have done so you can't do any acting and your fellow actors are also stalled. Similarly, work out the petty details of where you'll light the cigarette, sip the drink, and turn on the light switch. Any business that is contained within your actions and does not affect another's cues should be worked out completely outside rehearsal hours, as they're too valuable to waste on such details.

Think about your props. Will it help you to bring particular working props to the rehearsal? Why be dependent on the stage manager? If a particular purse, briefcase, or umbrella is essential to the correct timing of your business, bring one with you. The stage manager will be thrilled, the designer delighted to have a specific model of what he needs to find, and you'll make your own work richer. If the working prop is extremely valuable, you'll have to cart it back and forth with you, but if it is not, the stage manager will be happy to add it to his other working props and then to return it to you when the real props appear. The objects you handle while acting (and the unique way you handle them) are an important aspect of your performance. You can shape your performance by selecting your props.

Not all the work you do on your role is private. Some will bring you together with others. If, for example, you are in *The Contractor* and your role requires you to speak with a Lancastrian accent, you ought to engage a dialect coach. Or a juggling coach if you must juggle. Or a gymnastics coach if you must tumble. Or a singing coach if you'll be singing. There is no rule that states you must receive all your coaching from either the director or your mother wit. If the role calls for specific skills you'd be wise to seek the advice, training, and coaching of an expert.

And lastly, you can rehearse! Young actors sometimes have the impression they are not to rehearse outside formal rehearsals, whereas the truth of most commercial ventures is that you will have adequate rehearsal hours only if you and your fellow actors get together on your own and spend the time you need to prepare your scenes properly. These rehearsals can happen any place you have room enough to work in, and usually that will mean your apartment. So invite your partner over for dinner, and after dinner you can work. At least you'll develop a relaxed and friendly relationship with your fellow actors that will make formal rehearsals go well; at best you'll discover rich ways to play your scenes and develop a fine performance. In either event you'll protect yourself from the agony of performing when you are under-rehearsed.

Your work on yourself is equally important. Keep yourself rested, fit, and in top rehearsal condition. Get enough sleep, see a doctor if you feel a bug creeping up on you, don't waste your energy in excessive partying, and eat well.

Keep your head clear of unqualified good advice. Don't listen to your friends, your fellow actors, or your dear Aunt Nellie. Everyone will offer you advice. Every amateur will assume knowledge of what you do professionally, and you'll be told, "That's not how to hold a beer glass," "You have to trill your R's more when you talk Scottish," and "You know, of course, that Macduff has been having an affair with King Duncan." Avoid discussing your work with anyone not involved with the rehearsals. If you can't avoid it, just smile sweetly, say "thank you" for the advice, and forget it. You must become thick-skinned. Nothing disturbs a director more than the insecure actor who alters something from one rehearsal to the next and who, when asked about the change, replies, "They said it didn't look good the other way." There is no "they" qualified to tell you that. Not your coach, not your fellow actors, not even the stage manager or playwright. You may make changes you understand and believe in and for which you have clearly thought-out reasons. But don't think so little of your work that you'll follow the counsel of every self-appointed director you stumble across. Respect yourself and your director and that's all.

Finally, continue to live a non-theatre life. If only for one hour a day, forget the play and return to normalcy. Visit with non-theatre people whose lives, conversations, and interests have nothing to do with the theatre. You need the refreshment such encounters will offer you. You need the objectivity such returns to reality will make possible. If only for one hour a day, watch TV, play cards, read a book, or make love. You need the joys of a full life if you are to return to your arduous working day with a sane mind and a healthy body. If only for one hour a day, see something new. Go to a museum you've never visited, meet a stranger, eat an exotic dinner. You need the stimulus that takes you out of yourself and helps you confront the world again.

As I've mentioned, acting is like running. The sprint of performance requires weeks of training. The best actor, like the best runner, is best prepared for the event. The runner must know how to run and actors must know how to act. And then both must know how to work to ready themselves for the event. The runner must know how to train and you need to know how an actor behaves.

PERFORMANCES

Near the end of *Franny and Zooey*, J.D. Salinger's extraordinary stories about the Glass family, Zooey tells Franny about the theatre, about acting. Franny is despondent, desperate, and close to a nervous breakdown. She is repeating to herself the mystical Jesus Prayer and Zooey challenges her to tell him why: "I'd *love* to be convinced—that you're not using it as a substitute for doing whatever the hell your duty is in life." Zooey reminds her of their older brother Seymour's instructions that they should always perform well for the Fat Lady, and then he winds up his argument: "I don't care where an actor acts. It can be in summer stock, it can be over a radio, it can be over *television*, it can be in a goddam Broadway theatre, complete with the most fashionable, most well-fed, most sunburned-looking audience you can imagine. But I'll tell you a terrible secret—Are you listening to me? *There isn't*

*anyone out there who isn't Seymour's Fat Lady."** For all of us
actors, the Fat Lady is out there, at every performance. She is the
truest connection we can make. Communion with Seymour's Fat
Lady is what performance is all about.

Performances commence whenever an audience first joins your
play. You may have ten friends at a run-through, half a house at
a dress rehearsal, or three long weeks of paid previews, but the
same rules apply in every case. When there's an audience, there's
a performance. Your working habits and your behavior must
embrace the presence of that audience from the moment the first
stranger walks down the aisle to take a seat, for that first,
curious, and expectant viewer is always Seymour's Fat Lady.

The Daily Work Pattern

When should you arrive at the theatre? Equity stipulates a
half-hour call. That means you must be in the theatre and on the
job no later than thirty minutes before the curtain rings up. At
precisely that minute, the stage manager will take down the
sign-in sheet and if you have not signed in you are not in the
theatre. (*Never sign the sheet for another! That's a cardinal rule!*)
If you are not signed in, not on the job, the stage manager must
set into motion a plan which will lead to the show's going on
without you. While an A.S.M. phones to learn if you are on your
way or if you have met with an accident that explains your
absence, the P.S.M. instructs the company of the change to be
made. Costumes are hastily re-fitted for the understudy, the
conductor makes notations in his score, the follow-spot operator
prepares his changes, a sign is prepared for the lobby, and your
understudy goes through the agonies of the damned. And then
you saunter in ten minutes late. "After all," you explain, "I don't
even come on stage until thirty minutes into the show." You're
wrong. You may come on stage only thirty minutes after the
curtain rings up, but you come on the job thirty minutes before it
does. Your job and the jobs of everyone else in the production
depend on your being where you're supposed to be when you're

---

*J.D. Salinger, *Franny and Zooey* (New York: Bantam Books, Inc., 1969).

supposed to be there. And that means you must be signed in and on the job at half-hour.

As I write this I remember the time I missed my call. It was a summer season and Sunday performances began at 7 p.m. instead of the regular 8 p.m. I was doing Charles in my own production of *As You Like It* and as we played five shows in rotating rep we had never performed this show on a Sunday, so I had no established routine. I had an early dinner and decided I would go to the theatre early, get made up, and relax before show time—instead of rushing in at half-hour and being frazzled during my first scene. I sauntered into the dressing room to find a condition of panic. The stage manager was trying desperately to teach the wrestling match to a frightened and much too frail understudy, while his understudy (an inexperienced apprentice) was trying to learn the songs he would shortly sing as Amiens. Worse, the whole company was in a tizzy. If the director was so irresponsible as to be late might not the entire show be threatened? "The center will not hold " was the mood of the moment. I arrived, not sixty-five minutes early as I had believed, but moments before the lights dimmed and Orlando began, "As I remember, Adam. . . ." I apologized, got dressed, and went on. But I felt like an ass for days. And I can still recall the chills I felt nine years ago when I realized what I'd done.

You'll often wish to arrive at the theatre well in advance of the half-hour deadline. You may open the show and want ample time to do your warm-ups. Or you may have a complicated makeup to do. Or you may wish to go over your scenes on stage before the crews arrive to set up. In all such cases you are your own boss. Your employer only requires you to be in the theatre at half-hour. It's the Fat Lady who requires you to be there early enough so you can give her your best performance.

When you arrive at the theatre, you should be ready to go to work. That means you should have already done any warm-ups you can't do in the theatre, you should have cleared your head of your civilian life and worries, and you should be rested, well-fed, and wide-awake.

Immediately upon arrival, check the callboard. There may be information posted that will affect your work. A sign says there's a party after the show, so you can call your date now, rather than during the break between your scenes when you normally repair your makeup. Another sign tells you the costumes won't be back from the cleaners until twenty minutes before curtain so don't panic when you find yours is not in your dressing room. The callboard is your communications link to the production's administrators and it is your job to be informed of all notices posted on it. Only the stage manager or the company manager will post things on that board. It is not for your private use.

Now you're ready to prepare for your performance. If you need to warm up, now's the time. Vocalize where you can, do your body exercises wherever you're not in the way, but get your instrument warmed up. (As a rule, don't do these warm-ups in your dressing room if there's another place to work. Many actors don't like to listen to your gibberings, and you'll get along well with your dressing room companions if you avoid imposing on them.)

Once you're warmed up, go over any notes you may have received from the previous performance. These may have been given to you at the end of that performance by the production stage manager (or the director, if he's still around), or they may have been on the callboard when you came in. Make certain you don't make the same error two performances running. If a note affects someone you play a scene with, seek that actor out and go over it with him as well, so no one is surprised on stage during the performance.

Sometime during this pre-show period, check out your sets, props, and costumes. Don't get caught up short in the middle of the performance by the too-late discovery that the door on the set won't open, the apple you have to eat is rotten, or the mask you wear for the ball scene is missing. There are crews checking these items, and stage managers checking the crews. But errors do happen so you're well-advised to protect yourself by making a double check. But be careful of what you touch or move. The unions are very protective about who does what. If you find a problem, tell the P.S.M. Otherwise you may be the cause of a terrible ruckus and may even precipitate a strike.

Now put on your makeup. If you work in film or television, someone does this for you. It's quite pleasant and ego building to lounge in a barber's chair while a makeup man does your face. But if you work on stage, makeup is part of your job. You must know how to achieve the effects you desire and that means you must have studied makeup and that you must have practiced with it a great deal. Well before your first performance you should begin to work on your makeup as a portion of your homework. Dress rehearsals ought to be times for refinements, not beginning experiments. In most cases your makeup will be sufficiently simple and no problems will arise, but occasionally you'll have to wear a scar, false beard, wig, putty nose, or age makeup. When you design your makeup keep in mind that you'll be putting it on many times. Try to avoid details that take hours to apply and only "read" in your makeup mirror. Try to avoid prostheses which damage your skin and require you to alter your makeup from time to time. (While playing Macbeth I had a deep scar on my forehead which moved about from performance to performance so that I wouldn't damage my skin and create a permanent scar. I was young, then. That was a dumb thing to do. "Where will the scar be tonight?" became something of a company joke.) You have an obligation to yourself, your fellow actors, and your employers to do the same makeup each night. If you're in a long-running show, you'll grow weary of doing a complicated makeup and strive to simplify it. You'd be wiser to spend the time conceiving the easier one in the first place, during rehearsals. Then you'll be able to give the same face to your performance each time, and the Fat Lady will always be pleased.

Makeup supplies are your responsibility. A management may pay for unusual items like wigs or prosthetic noses, but you must supply everything else. You ought to have a well-supplied makeup kit. Metal fishing boxes are widely used as they have many compartments, making orderly storage of the varying brushes, tubes, pots, boxes, bottles, pencils, puffs, and sponges. Others use cosmetic cases made by luggage manufacturers. Others use shoe boxes and old plastic bags. What is important is not the container but the contents. You ought to have all the supplies and tools you'll require for a show. Those include scissors, tweezers, cotton swabs, hairpins, safety pins, sponges, powder puffs, nail files, nail clippers, hair curlers, hair driers, and other hardware and appliances that you might employ. In addition to the supplies you need to put on your face, you must provide the materials you'll need to take off your makeup. Whether you use cold cream, baby lotion, or soap and water, be certain you have the needed items. It is astounding how often actors will forget to bring cleansing tissues to the theatre. Well, a soft toilet tissue will work as a substitute, but the kind supplied in most theatre lavatories is coarse, so don't count on using it more than once or your face may break into a rash.

There are many unwritten rules of the dressing room which you ought to observe. Your performance and those of the people with whom you dress can be damaged if there is tension in a dressing room, so you should make every reasonable effort to insure that a cheery mood prevails. Begin by respecting people's time, space, property, eardrums, and superstitions.

If an actor near you needs the makeup mirror longer than you do (he has an old-age makeup to do, and he opens the show) give him preferential treatment at the mirror, the sink, and the lavatory. If an actor likes to go over his lines to himself while he puts on his makeup, respect his time, and don't interrupt.

In the crowded dressing room each actor strives to retain his territorial imperatives and these must be respected. Don't move someone's costumes and don't move his makeup equipment. And never muck with his good luck pieces, souvenirs, and totems. His chair is his chair and his space is inviolate. For some, performance is a combat with the unexpected and they need to approach it from the security of an ordered space.

An actor's property is equally inviolate. Don't use his makeup, tissues, cigarettes, matches, towel, hanger, or script without asking permission. If the response comes slowly, don't push the issue. An actor who is forever borrowing tissues, pencils, cigarettes, and change for the soft drink machine is an indescribable nuisance and quickly becomes a pariah. Similarly, protect your own property. You cannot be reminded often enough of this truth: *Something will be stolen on every show you work!* No matter the place, the time, or the people, something will be stolen. And the criminal will rarely be caught, because he is commonly among you—some member of the company. On occasions theatre robberies are outside jobs. A townie once cleaned out every wallet, watch, and purse from the dressing room of the Utah Shakespearean Festival while the entire company was getting notes on stage. (Despite the management's printed and oft-spoken admonishment to keep "valuables" away from the theatre.) But for the most part theatre thefts happen when many people are about and none of the perpetrators are strangers. You are well advised to leave anything valuable at home. If you must bring things of value into the theatre, leave them with the stage manager. Typically, the stage manager will make the rounds of dressing rooms shortly after half-hour and collect "valuables"— the watch you used to get you to the theatre on time and the money you will require to get you home again. These will be stored under lock and key until the end of the performance when they will be returned to you. Sometimes it takes longer for them to be returned than for you to get into street clothes, and your impatience may tempt you to skip this safeguard. You do so at your own risk. I normally keep my watch on. If I'm in a period show and can't wear it, I slip it up above my elbow. That way I can always know the time and be secure against theft. But I'd be equally wise to leave it with the stage manager. I know one actor who brings a "safe-hanger" to the theatre with him. It locks to a clothes rack, can be opened only with a key, and the key can be kept on his person throughout a performance. The "safe-hanger" has plenty of room for all his valuables. This is a particularly good acquisition for an actor who is on tour, likely to be moving from hotel room to hotel room, and who likes to travel with jewelry or other items which are small enough to be stored and valuable enough to be stolen.

Respect your fellow actor's sound tolerance. You like to talk loud and laugh and tell jokes to the ingenue in the next dressing room? Fine, except that you're driving to distraction the chap on your right. Many actors like a dressing room to be comparatively quiet. Not a library or a morgue, but not a high school locker room either. Try to get a sense of your roommates' attitudes and respect them.

Lastly, many actors have superstitions and can't abide singing or whistling in the dressing room. I once saw an actor rise in red-faced fury and threaten to punch a young man who was whistling quietly to himself as he applied his eyeliner. There is no accounting for the tensions many actors experience prior to a performance, so you must be on the alert. Complaints are commonly lodged against whistling, singing, raucous laughter, obscenities, and uttering lines from *Macbeth*.

☆ ☆ ☆ ☆ ☆

The stage manager gives calls over the loudspeaker, or by coming around to the dressing rooms: "Fifteen minutes," "Ten minutes," "Five minutes," "Places, please." It's time to perform. Your job requires you to give your best effort at each performance. Indeed, your contract stipulates quite precisely that you are obliged to duplicate your original effort at all subsequent performances. Your lines and line readings, blocking and gestures, interpretation and timing, relationships and rhythm must remain as consistent as your craft makes possible. If you change your performance inadvertently, the P.S.M. will give you notes, and if you don't respond he will call a rehearsal in which he will "take out the improvements." No one wants to come to the theatre for such a rehearsal, so try to respond to the notes you receive. If your continuing work on your role suggests a desirable change to you, you must go to the P.S.M. first and discuss it with him. If it does not affect another actor's performance, he may give you permission to make the change; and if he likes the adjustment, he may permit you to incorporate it into your standard performance. The decision rests with him. If your desired change is something that does affect another actor, he will discuss it with the actor in question, call a brief rehearsal for the two of you, if he deems it necessary, and then permit you to try it in performance. The P.S.M.'s job is to keep the show vital and if your change will help to achieve that he'll go with it. But his job is also to keep the show as the director left it, and if your change will distort the production, he'll reject it. Once the show opens, the P.S.M. becomes the arbiter of performances and his word is final.

To keep your performance at peak level requires great concentration and in a long run or in a stock situation where you may be exhausted after weeks of simultaneous performance and rehearsal, it is easy to let your energy slack, your concentration wander, and your performance slip. A common error is losing concentration on stage to the point that you forget your line or "go dry." Whenever that happens to you, and it will, you have only yourself to blame. Your concentration has wandered, or you've come to work ill prepared and you're doing your job poorly. You may be skilled at ad-libbing your way out of the situation, or you may be skilled at taking a prompt from the wings, but in any case you'll be sweating and your performance will suffer. I recall going "dry" in a performance of *Dear Liar*, the two-person play based on the letters of George Bernard Shaw and Mrs. Patrick Campbell.

There's no dialogue in the play, merely the exchange of correspondence, spoken out loud. Hence, there's no easy way to ad-lib and no way the other performer can help you out of a bad situation. I went dry, my mind raced in search of the correct line; my eye shot first across the stage to the actress, imploring her help, and then into the wings, where I saw the stage manager—my hope for salvation—flat on his back, asleep. Panic. Finally, the actress simply leapt to her next speech/letter and the performance lurched forward leaving the attentive audience more than a bit confused by the gap my "dry" had created. Most productions do not have a prompter and most actors prefer to work their own ways out of the occasional problem that arises, because prompters sometimes cause more problems than they solve. There's the tale, attributed to John Barrymore, of the moment in mid-performance when a silence fell on stage as an actor forgot his line. A low whisper from the wings. Nothing on stage. A low mumble from the wings. Still silence on the stage. Finally, from the wings, the very clear voice of the prompter gave the line so most of the audience could hear it and Barrymore turned to the wings and replied, "We know the line, dear, but who says it?"

Just as you may forget your lines if your concentration wanes, you may also miss your entrance. You must protect against this, and the easiest way is to build into your performance rhythm some exercise or preparation that takes its cue from a line of dialogue some sixty seconds before your entrance. That way you'll have to be in the wings, ready to come on, and you'll nearly preclude missing an entrance. Nearly, I say, because it's possible to be in place and still miss. I was in the wings chatting with an actor during that passion play done in Hollywood when I looked on stage and realized the man I was talking with had missed his entrance and that for about a dozen improvised lines the actors on stage had been looking towards the wings and sweating. I turned to my companion. "My God, Jack, you're on!" He smiled at me. "How am I doing?" he asked and calmly turned and walked into the scene. It must be the oldest gag in the business but it was new to me that night and I let out a sputtering, gasping laugh that must have sounded to the audience like someone in the wings was having a seizure.

Pranks are forbidden! Your job is to act well, not to try to make someone else act poorly. You owe the audience your best work and not your scorn. If you pull a prank, the Fat Lady will think as little of you as you apparently think of yourself. You will hear many stories of the "funny" pranks actors have pulled. Enjoy the stories, but don't add to them. There's the time the phone rang on a Broadway stage at a point in the action when no phone cue was planned. After the third ring the actors couldn't ignore it. The husband picked up the phone. "Hello? Yes? Oh, I see. My dear," holding out the phone, "it's for you." And there's the time I was doing the Inspecting Officer in a summer stock production of *No Time for Sergeants*. The action called for me to enter the latrine and inspect the toilets the hero had lovingly cleaned. From one to the next, in proper military fashion, I was to approach, bend over from the waist and look searchingly into the bottom of the toilet. Toilet number four revealed an 8x10 glossy of myself looking up at me. For some unknown reason I didn't break up. In character, I straightened up, turned to my guide and remarked "particularly interesting, that one." He broke up. We later laughed together. But we were both guilty of breaking the most sacred trust of the theatre—the trust of the actor and the audience. I tell the tale now with some amusement, but more guilt.

The final line of the performance is spoken and the lights fade to black. The audience begins to applaud and it is time for your curtain call. Many actors are made uneasy by curtain calls. Some feel naked without their characters to hide behind and don't like to present their private selves before the audience. Others have some sense of false modesty that argues their work doesn't merit a demonstrated approval. Others are so arrogant they feel the audience should be moved to silence, not applause, by their efforts. Or they feel a curtain call intrudes on the aesthetic experience of the performance. Regardless of the reason, they don't want to do a curtain call and therefore frequently do it badly. That is all unforgivable, self-indulgent nonsense!

The audience expects a curtain call. Since it's paying for this event, and since one part includes the curtain call, you have an obligation to perform it with the same professional seriousness you apply to all other portions of your job. The director directs the call. He dictates your characterization for the call (as yourself or as the character in the play), the blocking, the tempo, and the mood. Is it a joyous call in which you whoop as you stampede on? Or a stately and formal one in which you don't bow but merely walk into place and soberly stand as the lights dim again? Whatever, follow your directions. Play an action: to acknowledge the audience's applause. Curtain calls normally require you to move swiftly and with great precision. Don't talk to your neighbor, wink at a friend in the audience, show your contempt for your performance or the audience, or begin taking off your costume or your makeup. Respect your work and the audience sufficiently to do the call well. It is the final image the audience takes away with it. Do you want people to tell their friends to buy tickets to the show so you can continue to get your weekly paycheck? Then leave them with an image of your best professional manners. Do the curtain call with precision and energy.

Show's over. Time to leave the theatre. First you must strike your costume. Hang it up neatly and report any problems to the wardrobe department. Now strike your makeup. There are few breaches of professional behavior more obviously amateurish than that of leaving the theatre with your makeup still on or your hair still greyed from the white shoe polish you've applied to make you look old. Of course you want to leave swiftly, to join your friends or your guests and to get to the bar for a rejuvenating drink. But plan into your daily work pattern the time necessary to strike your makeup. Shampoo your hair, if necessary. If you were a mechanic who worked around and under cars all day you would scrub off the oil and grease before joining friends for dinner or a drink. Well, acting is just another job that gets grease all over you and it's wise to clean up before you leave the job. If you want people to admire you because you're an actor, act well, and they'll come to see your work. But don't advertise your profession to them in restaurants and bars. Those are not the places for you to seek the strokes your ego needs. Save your acting for the stage.

Before you leave the theatre, check the callboard for messages. You may be called for a photo session, an understudy rehearsal, or a costume fitting. Whatever is on the callboard, you're responsible for it. It must be your last stop on the job each day.

Opening Night

Your opening performance is the most important one you will give and you must focus all your energies on doing it well. The director will work to bring the entire production to a peak for "the night" and he may work to dissipate the unwanted rush of adrenalin which opening night excitement can produce by calling a line run-through or even a full dress rehearsal earlier in the day. He will attend to his job and you attend to yours.

Make certain you have rested well and that you are operating on real rather than nervous energy. Attend in advance to all the details of your social and paratheatrical life so you don't spend the final hours flapping about on tangential business. If you need a particular dress for the opening night party, get it days in advance. If you have tickets to deliver to your opening night guests, do so well in advance. If you have presents or cards to buy for people, do so before the final day. Opening night day ought to be lived as though it were any other performance day and the daily work pattern you've established ought to be followed so that you can arrive at the moment in peak condition.

In many companies, opening night gifts are a common cere-mony. Some actors give a token gift to everyone working the show—from star to doorman. Others give to their close friends only. Others give nothing. You may do whatever you wish, but be careful not to offend anyone. If you give a split of champagne to an old friend of yours, will that unnerve the actor who shares his dressing room and who has received nothing? Theatre people are cloyingly sentimental about opening nights and opening night gifts and the best guideline to your behavior I can offer is this—all or nothing. Either give a card and/or token gift to everyone, or give nothing. If you want to give a gift to a special few friends, do so outside of the theatre. Avoid creating an awkward scene. Actors arriving to their dressing tables on opening night can be very much like eight-year-olds in school on Valentine's Day. The number of cards each receives becomes important. The quantity of people who profess to love them is of more moment than the quality of that love.

Give the best performance you can.

Now celebrate. Begin by giving and accepting the congratula-tions which the company shares. At the inevitable party, be supportive, congratulatory, and cheery. Remember, everyone is as scared of the impending reviews as you are, and you all need to help buoy each other up. Have a good time, but remember you have a show the next day, so don't drink yourself into an oblivion from which you can't return in time for tomorrow's half-hour.

Now wait for the reviews.

Reviews

It is a sad reality of our commodity-oriented society that theatre reviews assert the influence they do. It is irritating to realize that audiences will respect the "consumer report" of a single journalist who may have shockingly little training in or sensitivity for the theatre. It is deplorable that so-so review from a powerful critic can lead a producer to protect his investors by closing a show after only one performance. It is a shameful reflection upon our public that they will respect the three-hundred-word opinion of an unqualified reviewer and not their own responses. Yet the sad reality remains: reviews influence the size of our audiences.

In a commercial venture, a show can close in one night if it is badly reviewed or run for three years if it is given raves. In an institutional theatre the reviews will have a less dramatic impact; the show will have its scheduled run, regardless. But the size of the audiences and (almost inexplicably) their enthusiasm will fall off if that reviewer doesn't like what he sees.

It is essential for you to judge your judgers. Who is writing the review? In some major cities there are some perceptive, informed, and literate critics. In most cities most reviewers are imperceptive, uninformed, and illiterate. This charge is made only because I've read reviews in dozens of cities in several countries over twenty years—and also because I've taught dramatic and theatrical criticism for a dozen or so years. I offer more than a sour-grapes opinion here. Too many of the reviews that appear in daily newspapers around the world are as foolish as this one from *The Advertiser,* the major daily of Adelaide, Australia.

Old-style theatre

The Murray Park Performance Group last night staged one of its largest productions—Sophocles' "Oedipus Rex."

As the play opened the chorus, representing the people of Thebes infested with the plague, dragged themselves about the stage and through the audience screaming for Oedipus to help them.

In true Greek theatre style, the play was performed on the steps in the centre of the College Playhouse, surrounded by the audience.

John Castle interpreted Oedipus on many levels—the questioning of his birth, the disillusioned discovery of his background, and the final banishment from Theban society because he was found guilty of the murder of his father so he could marry his mother.

The legend on which the play is based is old, strange and implausible, but nevertheless the Group did well to adhere to the dramatically right conclusion, as written by Sophocles, and not to introduce various neat and unconvincing "morals" that people have tried to import into his play.

                                                                              Miri Zlatnar

As an actor you know that your job, your career, and your ego are subject to the remarks of the reviewers. Attacks on your ego can be handled by judging your judge. Do you truly care what someone like Miri Zlatnar thinks of your work? Is Zlatnar's opinion any more valid than your Aunt Bessie's? The best way to deal with reviews is to ignore them. Don't read them. Don't let people read them to you. Don't dignify them with your attention. Unless you believe the critic is a qualified professional whose remarks might give you insight into your work, you are better off disregarding his existence entirely. I recall the late Michael O'Sullivan remarking acidly that he knew the good and bad parts of his performance and didn't need some refugee from the Obits Department to tell him his job.

Attacks on your employment can be combated in a different manner. If a production or a performer has been panned and if the show is not closing as a direct result, the company has an obligation to itself, its investors (or administrators if it's an institutional theatre), and its audience to give the best possible performance day after day. If you believe the critics and lose enthusiasm for your work, your performance will indeed become what the reviewers alleged—boring. But if you attack your work with energy and commitment, you may find that the audience does not share the critics' views and the word-of-mouth on your production may build you more good will than the journalist's column can destroy. The best way to deal with poorly written reviews is to denigrate them swiftly and then disregard them. Don't engage in lengthy gripe sessions with your friends. Don't dissect the reviews for their inanities. Don't question the function, literacy, or parentage of the reviewer. Just say firmly and briefly that you disregard the review and the reviewer and that you have better things to do with your time than to dwell on such inanities, and one of the better things is to get on with your job. Then proceed to do so, despite all supplications to join in the general lamentations. Your clear-minded commitment to your job can do more to improve company morale than any reasoned disputation with or about a reviewer.

Attacks on your own work must also be dismissed. You have only one recourse. Act well! The reviewer may be unqualified to judge your work, but you are equally unqualified to judge his. On rare occasions an actor or group of actors will foolishly engage a journalist in printed debate over his review of their work. Such an action is foolish for two reasons. First, actors are not qualified critics. You are not necessarily educated in dramatic theory, criticism, and aesthetics. Nor are you experienced in literary or journalistic writing. In short, if you write a letter to the editor, you reduce yourself to the level of the very writer you complain about. Second, you never saw the show he reviewed. You never entered the theatre, sat in your seat amidst a paying audience, and experienced the two hours of the event. All you know is what you imagine the show to be like, what you hope it is like, and what you intend the audience to experience. But the audience may be every bit as bored as the critic claimed. Or they may be in total disagreement with the critic. Or several critics may be in fundamental disagreement with one another. But one thing is true—you never witnessed the event.

What can you do? Act. If you've made the mistake of reading the reviews, extract any comments on your own work and consider their validity. Once in a while the reviewer will help you. If he says your accent is unbelievable, go find a dialect coach. If that professional concurs, work to correct that flaw in your performance. If the review says you are dull, re-think your performance beat-by-beat to consider if you're making choices that are both true and imaginative. If the review says you're not funny enough and a re-reading of the play convinces you that the character is not intended as a comic one, disregard that criticism. And if the critic is patently incorrect in other remarks, ignore him again.

The only assessment of your work that matters is the audience's. If the audience believes you, likes you, applauds you, you're doing your job well. If the audience likes you, you'll be hired again. Your reputation depends much more on the assessments that audiences and colleagues make of you than the one critics write of you. If you behave professionally and do your job as well as you can, you can dismiss the critics. I was being interviewed for an acting job once and the producer wanted to see my portfolio. "Do you have any reviews?" he asked. "Sure," I replied, "but I only keep the nice ones so I don't know what good they'll do you."

The Audience

How do you feel about your audience? Is it your father from whom you seek approval, your mistress from whom you want love, your enemy from whom you fear violence, your judge from whom you expect punishment, or your partner with whom you seek communion? For each actor there is a particularized feeling for an audience and that feeling will lead each to particularized behavior. Do you disdain your audience because you fear its judgment and as a result do you sneer during curtain calls? Do you lust after your audience and as a result do you hang around the lobby until half-hour in the hopes of being recognized or do you hang around the stage door following a show in the hopes of being congratulated? Are you afraid of your audience and do you bolt from the theatre when the curtain comes down and scurry home to the protection of your apartment? Whatever your relationship to your audience, you must understand its expectations of you and you must behave accordingly.

In performance the audience expects your best. It doesn't wish to see you fumble your lines, break character over a joke, or "phone in" your matinee performance. The audience has paid money and taken the trouble to come to the theatre to watch you be what it wishes it were. You must fulfill its need for fantasy. That is an unwritten part of the contract which is made when a ticket is purchased. A portion of that finest work requires you to feel emotions yourself—you must cry when your character cries and you must laugh when your character laughs. Through the miracle of *mimesis* the audience shares with you the emotions which you have as an actor, as you both become the fictionalized character. A communion is expected between you, and the medium for that communion is the character. You must both believe in it for the communion to be reached, for the contract to be honored, for the audience to be gratified. You will gain from the spirit and energy the audience invests in the character as it will gain from the spirit and energy you invest. In this happy instance the audience's need is your need. Its fulfillment is your fulfillment.

The curtain call is the mutual acknowledgement of that joint need and joint fulfillment. It is the ceremonial affirmation of the communion that was sought (and hopefully achieved). You bow to the audience in thanks for its contribution and it applauds yours. Like many ceremonies, this theatrical one is frequently empty, a vestigial reminder of what the theatre has been, can be. A bored audience claps out of a memory of previous fulfillments and a politeness supported only by habit. The actor bows out of civility and habit. But on occasions the ceremony is alive again and celebrates a communion that both actor and audience have relished. Angus Bowmer writes in his autobiography of the Oregon Shakespearean Festival about the rainy night when a devoted audience sat through a steady downpour to watch a performance. Afterwards, he recalls, the actors broke into spontaneous applause for the audience. Both had loved the event, shared in it deeply, and participated in its creation; both had found a ceremony through which to thank the other. It happened to me once. And maybe in each actor's life once is enough. I was performing Jerry in Albee's *The Zoo Story* under the direction of Gordon Heath. One performance was in the chapel of an old monastery in Royaumont, about sixty miles north of Paris. The audience was made up entirely of French students of American literature. At the conclusion of the performance, following the one scheduled curtain call, the audience began clapping in unison. A steady, rhythmic, incessant clapping. I didn't know what to make of it and was frightened. The clapping grew louder, more insistent. I looked across to the actor who played Peter as he stood in the opposite wing. He smiled, knowing the French custom. When a French audience truly likes a performance, it will clap in unison until additional bows are taken. It's like an Italian opera audience demanding an encore following an aria. Slowly, fearfully, I came out on the stage and joined Peter. We bowed. The clapping continued. We bowed again. I remember I was crying when I came off stage. What was shared at that moment is what the theatre can be and what an audience has a right to expect from each performance. We all know it happens rarely, but we must all work towards it. The curtain call is the shared moment in which we can jointly say thank you for the event or, at the very least, thank you for the effort.

Away from the theatre the audience expects you to be a member of its community. When you leave your job, return to your home, and go to your neighborhood shops you are just another worker. Your work may make you a public figure, recognizable to many, but you are also a part of the social fabric of your community. And you are needed. You help the image of the theatre and you add to the value of your own community when you put aside your defenses and those pretenses that separate you from your neighbors: when you become a "citizen-actor."

Paradoxically, your audience expects you to be forever a part of its fantasies, forever the character they saw you portray, forever the "artiste"—that romantic outsider. This is made clear when you consider the phenomena of groupies, autograph hounds, star gazers, and celebrity seekers. These are the avant-garde, the exponents of a general public interest, those who act publicly on the urges that more timid audiences repress. Your behavior to this part of your audience is an important aspect of your life as an actor.

I was standing with Richard Chamberlain one evening on the steps of a newly dedicated theatre in the small college town where we had gone to school a decade earlier. It was intermission of a student performance of Marlowe's *Dr. Faustus.* A small crowd of fans clustered about Chamberlain, seeking his autograph. How did he feel about all that, I asked. How did he feel about those intrusions on his privacy which stardom demanded. "It's all a portion of my job," he answered. "I earn my living from these kind people. I need them. I'm flattered they know me." I can't recall hearing a clearer explanation of the actor's obligations to his audience than Chamberlain gave that evening.

The public's admiration is not reserved for stars of Chamberlain's magnitude. Actors in school plays are greeted by strangers as they walk to their classes. Actors in summer stock are introduced to the druggist's children when they go shopping. At first you will feel awkward, embarrassed because you are being accorded attention you find disproportionate to your accomplishment, and piqued that your privacy has been infringed. But you must learn to behave correctly in these circumstances. You need those kind people, and they expect you to fulfill their needs as well. Be polite, modest, and warm. Sign an autograph for the child who asks. It is a portion of your job.

For audiences the theatre is a magical moment in which make-believe becomes truth and the fruits of its imaginations are given physical reality. In the anonymity a darkened auditorium creates, each individual adult merges into the collective child which is the audience—a child that willingly embraces the lies of the stage. In that magical time the actor is a wizard, an alchemist who makes that mystery happen. When the lights come up at the show's ending and the child diffuses into a crowd of individual adults, the magic has a residual influence. The adult never knew you, though the child knew your character. The adult knows you exist, knows you are not your character, but as he's never met you, he only sees and recognizes your character, which he knows as an adult does not exist. He carries this ambiguity with him from the theatre and when he meets you in his adult world he is confronted once again with his paradox. Are you Jack Nicholson or are you R.P. McMurphy? And, equally important, does he want to talk to you or to your character? You can help him through his puzzlement and get yourself out of a bizarre conversation if you consider in advance how to behave in such a circumstance.

Make the division between self and character clear immediately. Ask, "Have you seen me in anything else?" Or offer remarks like, "I found that role a rewarding one, but let me tell you what I'm working on now." Such opening gambits will make it evident that he's talking to you, and not the character, but that you are pleased he remembered your performance. Of course some of your audience will never make the separation, and for those you can only smile, be polite, and be brief.

Your Other Job

The show opened, the reviews were raves, and now you're settling in for a long run. For what may be the only time in your career you have a reasonable guarantee of a paycheck each week for months to come. And all for working only about twenty-five hours a week (matinees included)—and most of those hours in the evening. Time to take it easy. To reap the benefits of security and glory that your hard weeks of preparation have earned you.

Within two weeks you'll be bored to distraction! You'll have wearied all your friends with tales of your triumphs and you'll have seen every film in town and visited every theatre bar. Now what do you do? You get another job.

If you're doing stock or if you're working at a resident theatre, you already have another job. An acting job. While you do your eight performances each week, you spend your days preparing the next show. In the standard L.O.R.T. contract, management may work you up to 52 hours a week. That means you'll have your one day a week off—entirely to yourself. But you'll have rehearsals on each of the week's remaining six.

If you're not with a resident company, if you're on a production contract for a Broadway show, you've got some twenty-five or more hours a week to fill and you'll want to fill them constructively. You can take a job to earn money, you can seek additional acting jobs, or you can invest your time in the job of self-development—improving your skills, advancing your career.

You may need to take a job to earn money. "But I'm earning a handsome weekly check for my acting," you say? Not really. It's probable you're earning minimum or not much above it. At the time of this writing, Equity minimum on a Broadway production contract is $285.00. After deductions your weekly take-home will be about $197.00. By the time you pay your rent, buy your groceries, and pay your miscellaneous medical and clothing bills, you're broke! If you're careful, you can just get by on what you earn. But you won't have anything left over with which to pay back the debts you incurred looking for the job you now have. And you won't have anything left over to save against the day—not too distant—when the show will close and you'll be back pounding the pavements and knocking on doors.

Since you'll be available Monday through Friday (with the exception of Wednesday afternoon for the matinee), you can probably get a decent job. Actors commonly take jobs which permit them a lot of mobility, so they are free to shift if an audition comes up or a job develops. Typical jobs include waitressing, cab driving, sales clerking, substitute teaching, bartending, and office clerking—especially through temporary agencies. Depending on your skills, you can earn as much or more doing your second job as you will acting. And if you're practical, you can bank one entire check each week and build some security against the long hot summer when you fail to get a job in stock.

If money pressures are not too great or if you're a gambler and like to live on the edge of financial ruin, you may choose to seek a second acting job. For the most part that will mean short engagements in front of a camera—the odd day's work on a film, a week's work on a TV soap, a modeling gig, or the much-sought-after commercial. If your performance in the legit show is one that brings you good notices, or if you have a scene that presents you well (no matter how brief it is), you may try to use it as a springboard to other work. It is nice to make the rounds of casting directors and producers and leave invitations for them to come see your work. It is nice to mail out to any and all a postcard with your picture and vital statistics on it, encouraging others to seek your services. The fact that you're employed gives you an edge over all your out-of-work competitors, although it also puts constraints on your availability. Happily, most film and modeling work is somewhat flexible, and frequently schedules can be made compatible. I once performed two different plays in one day and crammed in the filming of a commercial between them. And my experience is in no way a unique one.

You may choose to spend your free time advancing your career by improving your skills. You may enroll in classes to develop your singing, dancing, or acting skills. You may use your present job to attract an agent (and that can be a time-consuming activity). You may turn your time and energies to other artistic vocations. Have you always wanted to find the time to write your novel? Complete enough canvasses for an exhibition of your landscapes? Prepare and record the demo which you hope will land you some nightclub and recording contracts? Well, now you have the time if you will use it, if you have the self-discipline.

The only thing you should not do with your free time is sit around and vegetate. Remember, time is our eternal enemy and you must use it wisely.

Touring

The romance of touring is one of the myths of the theatre. On late night TV you'll see Jack Carson films about the joys of the vaudeville circuit. Old actors' biographies will be filled with colorful tales of Des Moines and Duluth. At school you'll learn of Moliere's ten years in the provinces. And over a double scotch sour some friend will boast of his recent sexual conquests on the bus and truck tour of a ninety-minute version of *Oklahoma!* as it winded its way through college towns in the snow belt of upstate New York. And like all myths, there's a foundation of truth to it. Touring can be a rich and rewarding experience. It can also be a lonely, back-breaking exercise in artistic and economic futility.

If you get work as an actor, if you're one of the few members of Actors' Equity that makes a marginal annual income, sometime or other you'll go out on tour. If you're lucky, you'll go on the national company's first tour of a recent Broadway hit. You'll play extended runs in major cities and you'll travel by plane and train. But more likely, particularly in the beginning of your career, you'll stick your battered suitcase underneath your chartered Trailways bus and climb aboard for a smoke-filled journey from Trenton to Camden. Or worse, you'll sortie out of New York daily, by careening stationwagon, to three separate high school auditoriums. Wherever you're headed, there are some guidelines to behavior that can help make your tour a pleasant one.

The company manager will supervise your tour. He will accompany you from town to town and will be the producer's representative with the traveling show. He will attend to all travel arrangements, all hotel accommodations, and all personnel and financial matters. He'll get you your weekly check, arrange for a bank that will cash it, oversee all public relations calls, get you a doctor when you have an ache and a dentist when you have a pain. He'll arbitrate between you and another actor when there are personality conflicts and he'll arrange social receptions for you following performances. In short, he's your man on the bus.

You will not normally have any choice about travel arrangements. The company will travel together on common carriers. If a star is aboard, he may have contracted separate arrangements (first class on the plane or a private room on the train), but you should not expect to make private plans. If there is a day or two off in the middle of a tour and you wish to spend it away from the company (to visit family or go skiing), the company manager might discuss private travel plans with you. But his job is to insure that you are at the theatre each time, ready to perform, so if he denies your request for special treatment don't get angry. He's only doing his job.

Typically, the company manager will give you instructions about the quantity of luggage you may take with you. That is, the amount the management will pay to have shipped. You ought to travel as light as you can, since you don't want to spend your time, muscle, and money shifting unnecessary boxes and bags from bus to hotel to theatre to bus. While you may be on the road for an extended time and may want lots of changes for the varied occasions you'll experience, be advised against loading yourself down unnecessarily. Remember, in most towns you'll be new to the people you meet and the same outfit will suffice time after time. True, your fellow travelers will get to know your wardrobe intimately, but they'll be in the same situation. Besides, if you need a particular item, you can always pick it up along the way and mail it home when you no longer need it. The lighter you travel the happier you'll be. A good idea is to take one large suitcase and one ample shoulder bag. You ought to be able to carry your luggage yourself; otherwise the bellboys and redcaps will earn your salary.

While traveling you have the responsibility to be where you're instructed to be when you're instructed to be there. True, there'll be a lot of sitting around in bus terminals and hotel lobbies, but those hours are a part of your working week. Don't be the perennial latecomer who angers everyone. As with every other aspect of your working world, promptness is an essential courtesy.

The company manager will arrange your sleeping accommodations, but you may have some choices to make. Do you want to share a room to save money? Do you want a room with a private bath? Do you mind being fifteen minutes from the theatre if you save $5.00 a day or does walking home in the dark in a strange city frighten you? The company manager will have a variety of accommodations for you to choose from. But all of them will be expensive. Even in cities where you'll play long enough so that a weekly rate can be negotiated, you'll find you spend an alarming portion of your salary on your hotel room. But since you'll spend a lot of time in your room, consider how important it is to you and how much your personal comfort, your frame of mind and your work on stage will be affected by your choices. Are you, as I am, six foot three, and do you need a king-sized or at the very least a double bed (so you can stretch out diagonally)? Do cockroaches offend you? Or, are you happy in a YMCA dormitory? Whatever, make your choice wisely. Don't try to save $10 a week and make yourself miserable.

If you are with a tour that will spend many weeks in a particular city, you may be able to make private arrangements once you've arrived. You may want to move out of the hotel (even though a weekly rate makes it reasonable) and find accommodations of your own. The company manager may try to help you, but he may know as little about the city as you do, so be prepared to take care of yourself. Here's a good time to use friends. Have you acquaintances in the city? Have you friends in New York who have friends in the city you're playing or who have stayed there themselves on previous tours? Any source of information or advice is welcome. In some cities there are social organzations like "Friends of the Theatre" who will assist you. Or there may be another acting troupe in town. If it is a permanent company, the actors might be of particular service to you. But there are also agencies that help non-theatre people and you can try them. Travelers Aid and The Chamber of Commerce are frequently very helpful. Also, if the city has a college or university in it, the housing office may be of service. Indeed, many colleges will rent out available dormitory rooms at inexpensive rates on a weekly basis and those are always clean and comfortable.

"You are what you eat," goes the old adage. That is never truer than when you're on the road. If you try sampling the epicurean delights of each city you visit, or if you try to dine socially with the star who is earning five times your weekly salary, what you'll be is broke. If you try to live on candy bars, sodas, and the occasional pizza, what you'll be is fat. If you try to live on "fast food" what you'll likely be is sick.

If you're on the bus and truck tour making one night stands, you'll discover the job of finding a place to eat occupies a lot of your waking hours. Hotel food, as a rule, is overpriced. Cafeteria food is bland and, after a while, depressing. Chinese food is frequently inexpensive and a nice change of pace from the lunch counter meals which may be your norm. Wherever you eat, try to get some intelligent dietary balance to your meals. Some fresh fruit and an occasional salad may serve to keep your system functioning.

Of course what you want is a home-cooked meal. If you're adept at meeting people in strange cities, you may be able to wangle your way into their hearts and to their tables. Good luck. Your alternative is to cook for yourself. Most hotels will forbid cooking in the rooms. Most actors will cook in the rooms. How to do it? Quickly and "smellessly." An extraordinary ragout with chopped garlic in it may draw the management's attention, but there are times it's worth the gamble and there are other recipes that are less noticeable. If the management does come to the door . . . well, you're an actor, aren't you? Let's see that improvisation. Let's see that look of innocence that earned you the acting job in the first place. What will you cook on, you ask? You'll have to carry your equipment with you. An electric frypan is a first-rate substitute for a kitchen range. A picnic basket accommodates all the silver and crockery you might require. You don't want to pack and lug all that unless you're really going to use it, but if you're out on the road for many months, it may prove desirable. I know one actor who has constructed a most ingenious electric burner inside what appears to be a briefcase. He can pack it, carry it, and hide it from the night clerk with remarkable ease.

☆ ☆ ☆ ☆ ☆

The social crucible of a touring company challenges you daily. It is easy to make enemies and have a rotten time. It is easy to become a lonely stranger in a gabbling crowd. It is easy to become a social lion and lose all privacy. No one can provide you with guidelines to the happy life, but there are some questions you can put to yourself at various stops along the route, and the answers you come up with may help you to enjoy your trip.

Are you a part of a social clique? Are there actors on the tour that you like but rarely socialize with? It is likely you'll develop friends on the journey—your roommate, perhaps—but it is limiting if you see only the same, small group all the time. Cliques are divisive and the morale of the company and the quality of your collective performance may suffer if they become factious. Also, you'll find you're bored if you exchange thoughts and witticisms with only the same, small group day after dreary day.

Are the sexual or racial lines of the company too sharply drawn? Your social, political, sexual, and racial horizons might be constructively widened on a tour if you will take advantage of the opportunities before you. For once, you may not retreat entirely to the cocoon of your old friends and haunts. You must encounter new places and people; if you will relate to those people who share your traveling world, you can enrich yourself while you work.

Are you enjoying being a tourist? Do you get away from the theatre and the company enough to take advantage of the places you visit? It is easy to grow lazy on a tour and to miss out on the sights that you would otherwise travel miles to see and spend a fortune to visit. If you're in Philadelphia take in a matinee at the

Symphony, visit the Rodin Museum, and see the historical buildings. If you're in Seattle, run up to Vancouver on your day off. If you're in Los Angeles, get out of the bars and off the beach and see the Watts Towers or a bullfight in Tijuana. If you're in Washington, visit the Congress in action. In short, take advantage of this once-in-a-lifetime opportunity for a paid tour of faraway places with strange sounding names. That's the real excitement of touring.

Have you found a daily rhythm that makes you happy? Your schedule probably calls for you to sleep-in till mid-morning, eat breakfast at noon, go to the movies in the afternoon, have lunch at dinner time and dinner at midnight. But is your rhythm running you or are you living your life to suit your desires? You can get up at 8:00 AM if you want to, live the schedule the rest of the world lives, and go to bed shortly after the show comes down. It's up to you to control your world.

Do you enjoy your privacy? Do you have any privacy? If you are with the company too much you may feel stultified, restless. You must withdraw into yourself regularly. One of the touring actor's greatest challenges is finding within himself the resources necessary to fill the waiting hours that confront him. If you have no such resources, if you are dependent upon others for your fun, if external stimuli like television and card games are your only forms of recreation, you may be uncomfortable on a tour. Tours are filled with hours of waiting—no time for an outing or a formal gathering, just forty-five minutes after breakfast before the bus leaves. Do you know how to fill those hours? The actor who reads is usually the happiest. You'll be startled at the number of books you've always wanted to read that you'll now plunge through.

Are you able to make social contacts outside the company? On a tour you will long for a return to a non-theatre life, for conversations about anything other than the actors' gossip. If you are comfortable in a cocktail lounge, you'll probably have a place to meet strangers. In most cities there are bars that cater to traveling actors. Some are exclusively for actors, like the Variety clubs that you'll find advertised on the theatre's callboard. If you're even moderately religious, you may find social contacts through the offices of your church. That Sunday evening discussion group may be just what you need to meet someone—and who knows, you might get invited home to dinner. If you're attracted by intellectual environments (or by the attractive men and women who inhabit them), you might find the local college or university a good place to visit. If you visit the drama department, you'll find you're a celebrity—you're the thing all those students dream of being, a working actor. You'll meet people with common interests who think you're admirable. You'll find out about the good night-spots and cheap restaurants and you may even engage in a stimulating conversation or two.

But none of these will come to you. You must be the activist, the seeker. You can check into your hotel, eat in its restaurant, walk with your company to the theatre, and retreat to the hotel's television set after the show. Or you can tour. You can get out and learn about your country, your people, and yourself.

Closing Night

All good things must come to an end. Happily, some bad things come to an end as well. So whether you're closing a turkey before its formal opening or saying farewell to a show and a company that have been your delight and your life for over a year, you know that a life in the theatre is made up of short and intense episodes that all end. Whether happy or sad these final moments are charged with emotion and you can reduce your anxieties and discomforts by attending to many details in advance.

You may have business to negotiate with the management in advance of the closing. If you're closing on the road, you must ar-range return tickets to your place of origin. Here the company manager will assist you. If you've an interest in buying a part of your costumes from the management, talk to the company manager well in advance—so he can discuss it with the producer at a moment of relative leisure. You might like a dress, a suit, a raincoat, a pair of boots. Well, frequently the producer is happy to sell off those items for which he has no further use.

Your final exit from the theatre will be made easier if you cart away all your private belongings before the final show. If you've been in a run that is even two weeks long, you'll find you have extra street clothes (sweaters, raincoats, umbrellas), books and magazines, souvenirs and totems, and miscellaneous bric-a-brac in your dressing room. Take it home before that final day.

Leave your dressing room in good shape. Hang up your costumes neatly, clean up your makeup, and discard all garbage. Your job may be finished but there are some members of the company or theatre staff that still have work to do. Consider them, and show your affection and respect for them through to the final moment.

Say your farewells. Some of you will be sloppy sentimentalists and cry all over each other's lapels. Others will be lifelong enemies, glad they'll never have to see one another again. Others will be cool "professionals" and casually walk away from the theatre knowing that another job will lie ahead. However you behave, say your goodbyes. Include the stage management and the house crew (or stage door attendant). And say them briefly. Don't hang around hoping something magical will happen. Don't prolong your gloating over the show's failure or your tears over its final demise. Say "goodbye," hope you'll work again, and go.

Well . . . one final stop. Go out onto the darkened stage and silently say good night to the Fat Lady.

BETWEEN
ENGAGEMENTS

Acting is your hobby. Your avocation. The thing you do occasionally, when the circumstances permit. Oh, you may believe you're an actor and may tell others you're an actor, but are you? Compare your life as an actor to the life of a doctor, say. Or a fireman. Or any of those who practice what our society calls a profession—a vocation that requires extended training, that deals in social services, and that is highly remunerated. Ask yourself how much you earn and what proportion of your total earnings comes from your acting. Ask yourself how extensive your training has been and what licensing or standards of excellence are required by the acting "profession" (are they comparable to those required of a C.P.A., for instance?). Ask yourself how much time you spend acting. If you become a pharmacist you'll spend 40 hours each week, fifty weeks a year or 2,000 hours a year at the job. If you're lucky as an actor you may work 50 hours a week 15 times, or about 750 hours a year. Oh, you may be qualified to be an actor, and you may want to be an actor, but in all probability acting is your hobby. Your avocation. The thing you do occasionally, when the circumstances permit. What do you do with the rest of your life? What do you do "between engagements?"

A portion of your life as an actor is spent in preparing to act. The rest is spent in non-theatrical pursuits: earning enough money to live, meeting your obligations as an individual, as a member of a family, or as a citizen of your country. Let's take a look at your life.

Training

Training for acting is a lifelong pursuit. Before you ever embark on an acting career you must seek some basic training. You must have modest control over your body and voice. You must have the ability to concentrate. You must have a method for recreating physical and emotional states in yourself. You must have some method for analyzing a text. You must have some ordered methodology for rehearsing—for preparing a role. You must have some beginning grasp of the techniques required on a stage or before a camera—the modes for communicating what is thought and felt. You may announce yourself as an actor without these skills. Thousands do so annually. But if you are serious about a career in the theatre, if you hope to make acting your profession instead of your hobby, you must have some basic training. There exist three common channels for beginning training.

The first of these is amateur theatre experience. This first exposure to acting—be it in a church group's annual presentation, a community theatre's production, or a school play—is the least effective, but the most widely practiced form of training. In such circumstances you will learn by doing. You will "jump in the deep end." Commonly, you will learn from those who are more experienced than you and you are in danger of learning their bad habits. You'll learn to reach for effects rather than to create truths. You'll learn a set of mannerisms instead of a way to produce behavior. You'll learn some tricks by which to fool an audience rather than a way to share your experience with it. If your training is limited to amateur performing, you may find you're limited in the various kinds of acting you can do as well as in the qualitative level at which your work is acceptable to an audience.

The second channel for acting students is the theatre school— either a conservatory like London's Royal Academy of Dramatic Art, or an institutional program found at so many American colleges and universities. The quality of the hundreds of programs in this category varies widely. One measure of that quality is duration. A three-year program is superior to an eight-week crash course. Another measure is admission standards. A program that selects a small number of students, by audition only, is superior to a program that advertises on matchbook covers and accepts anyone who can pay the tuition fees. A third measure is the curriculum. Programs with a variety of teachers presenting a variety of classes are superior to programs with only one teacher. Another measure is the credentials of the faculty and the location of the school. A program with a faculty that has no professional credentials and no professional contacts and that is far from a major theatrical center is inferior to a school, like the Juilliard School, for example, that has a large faculty of working professionals and is located in New York City. Each school has its own philosophy, focus, and methods, and you may have trouble discerning which is the best one for you. But if you are planning to invest three years of your life in formal training, you are advised to make your selection carefully. Visit the school if at all possible. Read all available literature about the program, facilities, location, faculty, and alumni. If you aspire to join a resident theatre somewhere in a large city, you don't want a rigorous preparation for what has come to be called the Alternative Theatre. If you want to be a movie star, a program based in classical dramatic literature is less valuable to you than one focused on the skills necessary for a career in "show business." You can usually discover the right school (or schools) for your needs through reading, talking with the schools' representatives, or through the good offices of your teachers, directors, and friends. The only advice it might be proper to offer is this: don't practice false economy. Don't choose a program because it is less expensive or shorter. Choose the *best*.

The third channel is private study with a master teacher. The same commonsense guidelines you would use in picking a training school pertain to this. The teacher in New York or Hollywood is likely to be of more use to you than the teacher in Las Cruces, New Mexico. (There will be exceptions to every rule. Generalities, however, are the only currency I can deal in here.) There are two additional concerns. Each teacher has particular skills—what do you wish to learn? The teacher of tap is not necessarily a good teacher of classical ballet. The teacher of singing is not necessarily a qualified teacher of voice production or dialects. The teacher of Stanislavskian emotional recall may not be the teacher you need for lessons in the spontaneous improvisation best taught through theatre games. You must choose your teacher for what you wish to learn. The teacher's personality is the second concern. You will not learn equally well from all teachers. That is no reflection on their abilities or yours. It is merely a human truth.

☆ ☆ ☆ ☆ ☆

When you have completed whatever basic training you pursue, you are ready to begin looking for work and to begin the rest of your training—the training you will work at between engagements for the remainder of your life as an actor. In Hollywood, New York, London, Toronto, Sydney, and throughout the acting world, actors are taking classes. Usually from master teachers and with particular goals in mind: skills, training of the instrument, developing a system of work, scene-study classes.

SKILLS   The more things you can do, the greater your chances for employment. Many actors spend a sizeable portion of their time and available funds in expanding the repertoire of their skills. All manner of dance classes, music lessons, singing classes, circus technique classes, dialect classes, audition technique classes, modeling classes, combat classes, mime classes, and paratheatrical classes like yoga, T'ai Chi, and Transcendental Meditation are energetically pursued by aspiring actors.

TRAINING OF THE INSTRUMENT   Some actors will pursue classes to correct deficiencies in their training or to maintain their levels of accomplishment. Actors without satisfactory vocal instruments may study to achieve good breathing habits, strong breath support, enriched resonances, or unlocalized accents. Others may wish to correct minor speech imperfections such as lateral or sibillant lisps. It is also common for actors to enroll in programs of physical workouts at the gym—to achieve or maintain a strong and well-toned body.

DEVELOPING A SYSTEM OF WORK   Too many actors leave their basic training without a clearly defined and readily implemented system of work. They are without the tools they need to analyze a script or prepare a role. These actors study with "acting" teachers. In every major theatre center there are teachers who conduct weekly or twice-weekly classes in which students can learn how to approach a role and how to prepare a role. Most of these classes are taught by successful actors who have evolved for themselves a method of work which is almost always some variant on the Stanislavsky system. Fads for these teachers come and go, and each season actors will try to study with the teacher who has helped someone become a success the preceding year. Sanford Meisner one year, Uta Hagen the next, Jeff Corey the year after. Those who have endured for several years and who have earned the respect of the profession (as have the three listed here) are much in demand and take students by audition only. There are always new teachers, though, and sometimes they are good.

With "acting" teachers more than any others, compatibility is essential to effectiveness. If you get along well with the teacher, great. Many will function as gurus and expect your devotion. If you can't find it in yourself to give it, try a different teacher. It would be nonsense to suggest that one of these teachers is demonstrably superior to another. It would be safe to assert, however, that *you* will connect better with one than another. Happily, you have the chance to experiment. Unlike the university or conservatory to which you commit yourself for a period of years, most acting teachers will take students for six to twelve weeks at a time. If you find one you like, you can continue in his classes for years on end. If you want to shift to another, you can do so easily.

SCENE-STUDY CLASSES   You like to act. You wish to act. You need to act. Well, if nobody has hired you recently, you're not acting. And your acting skills are like the runner's skills—if you don't use them regularly they go stale. How can you hope to demonstrate your sensitivity and versatility in an audition if you haven't acted in several months? The answer is that you must act in classes. You need to maintain or sharpen your acting craft by doing it regularly, and the "scene-study class" is the most common place for actors to do this. There is a cruel irony here. You are a professional because people will pay you to act and you're reduced to paying someone for the right to act. In New York there are countless scene-study classes and serious actors attend them with regularity. The best known are probably those of the Actors Studio and the H-B Studio, for in those select locales some of America's best known actors keep working at their craft. In Hollywood the common form is the "workshop" or "showcase" theatre. There are actors who pay $40 a month for the opportunity of getting together to act—frequently without the supervision of an important mentor, as in New York. (True, the Hollywood workshops provide showcases which the actors hope will lead to their getting employment, but they also provide the only chance many have to act for months at a time.)

The problem of finding good instruction is as much a part of the actor's continual nightmare as the problem of finding good audition pieces. You'll rarely be completely satisfied. You'll continue to explore, looking for that teacher who will hold the secret you believe you need to become a star. Well, while looking, where do you begin? Teachers in New York and Hollywood advertise in the trade papers—*Variety, Back Stage, Show Business, Hollywood Reporter.* You will probably seek the advice of friends, the agent you're hoping will sign you, or someone who has studied with the teacher you're considering. Frequently these teachers have an arrangement by which you may visit and observe on one or two occasions before you must either pay to stay or leave. Finding a conservatory program is equally difficult. Begin geographically. If you're English, go to London and if you're Australian stay down under. It used to be fashionable for American students to go to London, but in the past decade a number of fine conservatories have developed in the States, and also young actors returning to New York from London have discovered they developed no contacts during their two or three years abroad and were correspondingly disadvantaged. Within the

States you will either go to the Northeast (Washington to Boston) or to whatever region of the country you live in—if there is a decent school in that area. Good information can be sent to you by the offices of The League of Professional Theatre Training Programs or The University Resident Theatre Association. The former has offices in New York and the latter in Washington; between them they represent all the university-connected training programs in the country. The New York-based conservatories, like the Juilliard School, the Neighborhood Playhouse, and the American Academy of Dramatic Art, all advertise in the trades, and in such theatre journals as *The Drama Review* and the *Educational Theatre Journal,* copies of which you can locate at any library.

☆ ☆ ☆ ☆ ☆

No matter where, no matter with whom, and no matter how long, you must study. As the dancer must study the dance and the violinist must study the violin, the actor must study his craft. The road to success is littered with the corpses of those who believed in shortcuts.

Not all of your training happens under a teacher's guidance or in a formal class. Just as you are on your own when the performance begins, you are on your own for a large portion of your training. You will need a clear program for self-instruction and a lot of self-discipline. But if you are to be the actor you wish to be, you will have to spend some portion of each day in concentrated self-instruction. You will succeed best if you regiment yourself and spend the same time on this work each day.

To begin, you must exercise your voice and body each day. If you've been well trained, you should know a set of exercises you can employ. If you spend 10-15 minutes on your voice, it will serve you well when you need it. The same applies for your body. Many actors use standard conditioning exercises; the best are those outlined in the handbook for the Royal Canadian Mounted Police. Again, 10-15 minutes before bed or upon arising will help you immeasurably.

Acting is an imitation of human behavior and you can broaden your understanding of human behavior by studying the other arts. Take advantage of the museums, galleries, concerts, sculpture exhibitions, dance concerts, operas, and movies that are available to you. Any week that goes by without your visiting a museum or hearing a concert or seeing a classic film is a wasted week. You will act Shakespeare better if you have heard a concert of madrigals. You will act Sam Shepard's plays better if you have seen an exhibition of Andy Warhol's canvasses. To act Beckett well you must first have walked among Giacometti's sculptures.

You can't always get out to a museum, but you can read every day. Most actors in America today are sadly uninformed about the literature, history, and practice of the art they aspire to serve. The only explanation for that is their own sloth. There is no justification. Yet there's so much to read. Where should you begin? By imposing some sort of plan and schedule on your reading. For example, plan to read a play every single week. Plan to read a book about acting every month (a biography of an actor, a study of some theory or style, a history of the craft). Plan to read a book about the history or practice of theatre each month (a discussion of Shakespeare's theatre, a history of the Federal Theatre Project). Subscribe to theatre journals like *Plays and Players* or the *Drama Review*. In short, set yourself some categories and some goals. One way to help yourself stick to your schedule is to create a discussion group. Select a handful of your professional colleagues who agree that such a plan is a desirable one and meet once each month to discuss your joint reading. If you screen your members carefully, you'll find the discussions stimulating. If this system does not appeal to you, create your own reading list. Or get one from some university's theatre department. If you write to a reputable department and ask for their Ph.D. reading list, you'll get several hundred titles you can select from.

☆   ☆   ☆   ☆   ☆

Go to the theatre! I am disturbed when I talk with actors or acting students and discover how rarely they go to the theatre. I may overreact to their seeming disinterest, but I am suspicious of actors who don't go to see another actor's work. There is much to be learned from watching a brilliant performance and something to be learned from every production you see—even if only negatively. See how another actor confronts particular problems. How would you have dealt with that scene? That monologue? That prat fall? Doctors have operating theatres in which they learn by watching other doctors at work. Football players screen films of other teams' games. You should see as much theatre as you possibly can.

See performances more than once. I am continually puzzled by actors who go to the theatre only for pleasure. You should also go to learn. To watch, consider, assess, and learn. The best learning is by comparison. Go see that intriguing performance more than once. See more than one actor in the same production. (Is Burton's *Equus* different from Perkins's, Hopkins's, or Bedford's?) Don't ask if it is better or worse. But is it different? And if so, how? And why? And what would you do if you landed that role in summer stock two seasons from now? And how will you do it in scene-study class next month? Think of the many recordings of a Beethoven symphony you might listen to. That's how many variants there can be on a performance. You can learn from all.

"But it's expensive," you moan. True. But can you afford *not* to go? Isn't that a more serious question to pose than, "Can I afford to go?" There are some ways to reduce the expense, however. In New York the Equity office distributes free tickets to shows every day to card-carrying members. If you know people working on a show and if you select a slow night, Tuesday for example, the company manager or stage manager might be inveigled into "walking you in"—bringing you through the stage door and into the auditorium, to occupy an empty seat as the house lights dim. There are also reduced rates for New York tickets now available through the Theatre Development Fund (TDF) booth at Duffy Square (47th St.). And, if all else fails, you can "back in" at the intermission. True, you'll miss the first act, but if your goal is to learn by observation, seeing part of the performance is better than sitting in the bar having another drink. All you do is inquire at the box office what time the intermission begins, stand outside, and as the audience filters out, you filter in. Once in, wait until the house lights dim for the second half of the show and either grab any empty seat or stand at the back. Once in a while you'll get caught and ejected, and your pride may be bruised, but mostly you'll spend an hour or so studying your profession—for free.

Looking for Work

Most new actors in New York and Hollywood suffer from acute cases of the "upfers," a disease endemic to the acting profession and one which strikes young actors with its most virulent stain. The symptom is heard in every bar, coffee shop, waiting room, and party where actors gather. "I'm upfer a role in that show." "My agent is sending me upfer a commercial next week." "I was upfer that pilot, but it didn't sound right for me." The cause of this disease is the actors' need to feel a part of the profession which he senses is happening all around him but which he is not yet actively practicing. Actors feel a need for self-delusion. If they can persuade themselves that employment is imminent, they can imaginatively project themselves to the enviable role of a "working actor." They have tired of that other self-delusion by which young actors proclaim they are not interested in commercials, or television, or repertory, or musicals, or whatever is the form of theatre employment under discussion—which by coincidence they have not yet been asked to do. They have come to accept the salty veteran's explanation that there are only two kinds of actors—those who get work and those who don't. There is only one cure for the "upfers." Employment. In the parlance of the medical professional, employment is a miracle cure. One injection and the "upfers" are over. At least for a while. It is a recurring disease.

How do you get that employment? That cure? Well, the first problem is to locate the clinics where it is dispensed. Once there you can follow the established ceremonies of auditions. But you've got to find out where to go, first of all. There are public channels and private channels.

The public channels include all published notifications of interviews and auditions. In the New York and Hollywood Equity offices there are callboards which list all upcoming auditions for stage work. Equity requires an open call for every show under its jurisdiction. These are general calls and frequently they turn out to be cattle calls, but the information posted is accurate and actors will be seen and, despite rumors to the contrary, actors do occasionally get hired from open calls.

The trade papers (*Variety, Hollywood Reporter, Back Stage, Show Business*) also list casting news, and frequently the concise notices at Equity are fleshed out in the trades with descriptions of the types being sought, names of directors and writers, projected opening dates, etc. The trades also have listings for non-Equity jobs—showcases, non-Equity stock and dinner theatres, commercials, and TV and film jobs. Information in the trades is not always accurate but you have to follow it up anyway. Sometimes the press release a producer has sent to a trade is printed too late to do you any good. On other occasions the show has been entirely or largely cast and the notice is the producer's way of meeting his legal obligation to Equity. But sometimes there are "jobs in them thar hills" for actors who will prospect long enough and hard enough.

Most hiring for the regional theatres is done through the offices of the Theatre Communications Group. This Ford Foundation-supported organization has offices in Manhattan and coordinates auditions for the directors of theatres across America who come to town to locate actors. TCG holds general auditions periodically to swell its files and you ought to inquire how and when you can audition for its casting directors.

Casting notices for store-front workshops in New York frequently never reach such formal publications as the trades. Scribbled notes on the callboards of bookstores and bars, two printed lines in underground newspapers, and notices posted on the doors to lofts and workshops are sometimes your only way of learning of auditions. As you can't possibly cover all the bases you might like to, you'll have to be selective, and you'll find you rely heavily on word-of-mouth.

Word-of-mouth is the most common source of information about auditions. It stands to reason, then, that the more people you talk with and the more places you circulate, the better will be your chances of finding that audition which will ultimately lead to your landing a job.

Your contacts are your major suppliers of information. The best contacts are those who are a bit more experienced than you, and these are frequently found in your classes. If there were no other reason for taking dance lessons and scene-study classes than to learn about forthcoming auditions, the money you'd pay would still be well invested. One way of choosing a teacher might be to investigate how many of his students work with any kind of regularity.

Another source of contacts is the "old school tie." If you have gone to Carnegie-Mellon, or Yale, or the American Academy of Dramatic Art, or any of the many other schools in operation a long time and whose students have been out in the business for some years, you can seek some assistance from them. You are usually sufficiently younger not to be their competition and there is a sentimentality that guides us to help our schoolmates.

A major source of information is the informal exchange that happens at theatre bars. (This is much truer in New York than in Hollywood where distances are so great that actors don't gather with the same regularity as they do in Manhattan.) For each level of theatre, there are different bars. Broadway theatre is served by a network of restaurants and bars in the theatre district: Sardi's, Charley's, Downey's, Joe Allen's, Jimmy Ray's, Backstage, and a few others. The downtown theatres of off-Broadway and off-off-Broadway also have their haunts. It will behoove you to make the rounds of these watering spots with some regularity. I'm not suggesting you become a bar-hopper and spend each evening panting desperately from stool to stool trying to overhear secrets that will make you a star on the morrow. I am suggesting that these are the places where you can meet your friends casually and where you can learn from each other.

Parties are fine ways to meet people, develop friendships, and learn about employment possibilities. Not all of you are party people, however, and if you are a stay-at-home type you can help yourself by considering parties a portion of your job—as significant as reading the trades and making the rounds. Go when you can—you may do yourself some professional good. And once in a while you might even enjoy yourself.

One of the least enjoyable and most tiring ways of looking for work has been dignified with a lot of romantic jargon. You'll be told to "go out on the street," "pound the pavement," and "make the rounds." These are all elegant ways of saying that since no one will come looking to hire you, you've got to do the looking. It means you must walk into as many offices as you can. Agents' offices, casting dirctors' offices, producers' offices, television programs' offices, theatre managements' offices. Anywhere you can find someone to whom you can present yourself. It can be embarrassing to make the rounds for days on end and never get past the receptionist. It can be demoralizing to pound the pavement for days on end and receive nothing but rejection. "Nothing today." "We're not casting anything this month." "Mr. Jones doesn't ever hire your type." "We only see people submitted by agents."

The phrases vary but they all boil down to a simple "No! We don't want you!"

Enterprising actors before you have made your task easier by cataloguing the names and addresses of most producers, casting directors, agents, television network casting departments, advertising and modeling agencies. You can get most of these at the Drama Book Shop, 150 West 52nd Street, New York City. Some are collated alphabetically, but at least one is done by address— so you can go from building to building and save yourself a great deal of time and shoe leather. There are also lists published by the unions (Equity, AFTRA, and SAG) and by theatre agencies like TCG.

Just as actors suffer from the "upfers," employers suffer from "short memoryitis." That agent you left your photo with two months ago has no idea who you are today. The director who told you he liked you but had nothing for you in the show he was casting no longer knows your name. If you hope to work as an actor you must continue to look for work throughout your entire career. I was seated in a filthy waiting room in New York, readying myself for an audition for a show to be presented in Philadelphia (where I lived, but where no auditions were being held). Alongside me was a student of mine, a young actor on one of his first auditions. Across from us was an old actor, perhaps in his mid-sixties. His turn came and he went in to the audition. The young man turned to me. "Is that me in forty years? Will I still be waiting in cold hallways, trying to find six weeks' work out of town?" "If you're good enough to make it," is all I could reply. "If you've got the stamina and the resilience. And if your need to act is strong enough."

You can keep your name before potential employers in several ways. As suggested earlier, you can create a mailing list of all your contacts and send periodic reminders of your availability. These are most attractive if they announce that you are presently working, or can be seen soon on such-and-such a television show. You can also make the rounds of offices with some regularity, as a live presence is more influential than a mailer.

One final thought about looking for work. The telephone is your best friend and constant companion. You must have both a phone and a twenty-four hour service. You need to be able to call people and they must be able to call you—even if you're not at home. If you have found out about a job, done an audition, and sold yourself successfully, you don't want to lose out just because you're not at home when the casting director calls. You need either an answering service or an answering machine. The machine is perhaps preferable, as it takes the entirety of the message instead of only the essentials. Also, you can leave a brief recorded greeting and message on the tape so that callers will know they have made contact with you. Sophisticated equipment permits you to call in to your machine from any phone and the machine will play back for you the messages it has taken during your absence. But these machines are expensive, and you might not be able to afford one right away. A quite acceptable alternative is to engage an answering service—either a separate number that people can call to leave you messages, or a service that is hooked up to your own number so that someone will pick up your calls after the third ring. The advantage of this system is that you can instruct the service to give callers the number where you can be reached, if you're not at home. As many of the operators working for the services are unemployed actors, they are usually efficient, polite, and concerned for your career. The fee for an answering service varies in relation to the services rendered. Some are not open 24 hours a day; others will not forward messages; others will not trace you even if the call is work-related and urgent. The monthly fee is usually between $5 and $15, and you get what you pay for. There are many to choose from, and ads in the trades will give you details on several.

Looking for work is a fulltime job. You can make the rounds each day, seek out your contacts each night, go to classes, read the trades, stop by Equity, and hit every audition you can get into. And you still may not find work. Common sense will tell you that the harder you look the greater will be your chances of finding. And that would be true, if all other things were equal—which they aren't. The theatre is an unfair business in which jobs are granted to friends, sex objects, freaks, and occasionally to the most qualified candidate. Since the grounds for qualification are largely subjective, it's hard to measure your successes and your rejections. But one truth remains immutable. *You cannot get a job unless you look for one.* I see many cases of so-so actors who work steadily because they are terrific job finders. I also see the opposite—talented and trained actors who don't work because they can't locate the jobs. Your career is very much yours to control. Follow your own best urgings.

Agents

The beginning actor believes an agent is the key to success. The working actor thinks he is a necessary evil, a parasite who gets paid for doing nothing. The successful actor's agent may be both a friend and business advisor. For all actors the agent is a puzzlement. Objectively, he's a guy trying to make a living by rendering services. What do you pay him to do?

You pay him to find you work. He will apply himself in direct proportion to his possible earnings. If you're a beginner he knows he can't make much for his services, so will probably spend very little time on your behalf. Since you're not likely to earn more than minimum at the beginning of your career, he can't expect to earn anything. If he works to get you jobs, it's in the hope that one day you'll be a big earner and he'll have invested his time wisely.

You pay him to negotiate contracts for you. This he will do responsibly, and you can trust him to get as good a salary for you as can be hoped. Your contract includes more clauses than the basic weekly pay, of course, and these items the agent is particularly skilled at negotiating: residual fees, raises after a specified number of weeks, vacations, billing, out clauses, fees for recordings, percentages from endorsements, etc.

You pay him for professional advice. He can advise you on your image, about photography, jobs it is wise or stupid to accept, showcases to perform, audition pieces to prepare, and a thousand other items ranging from advice on your income tax return to parties you should attend.

In New York an agent is less significant to the beginning actor than in Hollywood. If you are headed for New York, you can get a list of all authorized agents from the Equity office. If you desire an agent, select a few names from that list and send them your photo and resumé, with a covering letter explaining that you have just arrived and will call their offices in a few days to seek an appointment. Follow up that letter with a call. You'll get the receptionist. Perhaps she'll tell you to come for an appointment, but more often than not she'll say that the agent is "not taking on any more clients just now," or that he "asked me to tell you that any time you're in a show you should let him know and he'll try to come see it." If you get a warmer reception than that, you are fortunate indeed.

At some point you will be admitted to an agent's office. Perhaps he has seen your showcase performance, or perhaps he's in a slow season and can take time to look for new clients. Once there you'll learn that he is not interested in signing you to an "exclusive" contract, but that he'll send you up for things and be happy to represent you on any job you find yourself. That's useful to you, as you can now tell people at an interview that they can call your agent, Joe Doakes, if they'd like to engage you, and they will infer you are worth hiring, because why else would Doakes bother with you? It is common for you to have informal working relations with several agents at once. Typically, one will handle TV and film work, another commercials, and a third will focus on stage work. But those divisions are arbitrary and no general rules apply.

Any time you get a job that an agent has sent you to, he will claim his percentage. Any time you use the agent to negotiate a contract for a job you found yourself, he will claim his percentage. But you are free to negotiate any jobs on your own and the agent has no claim on you.

If you begin to get work regularly and the agent believes your income will be sufficiently large that his percentage will be worth his while, he may try to sign you to an exclusive contract. That means only that you may not employ other agents and that you must give your agent his percentage on all work you do. He will negotiate all of your contracts, even if you continue to find much of the work yourself. The only reason you would sign such an agreement is if you believe he will work hard to find you work. As his income is dependent on yours, he probably will, but if he doesn't your agreement can be cancelled after a specified time, so check that clause with great care before signing. Know how to get out of a bad situation, and know equally the ease with which the agent can drop you.

If Hollywood is your destination, different guidelines apply. In the TV and film world all contracts *must* be negotiated by agents

and a very high percentage of all work is secured through agents.
(True, you may still ferret out jobs on your own, but the agent will
enter into the negotiations early and will work with you to land
the job.) While in New York you might go for years without even
trying to get an agent, in Hollywood you must sign with one
before you can hope to work.

Hollywood agents are in a position to gamble on newcomers
more often than New York agents because of the huge salaries
that are paid to film and television actors and because acting
skills are less significant to your potential employment than your
personality and bone structure. As a result, it is not too difficult
to get an appointment with an agent on the West Coast. But that
agent will want to see something of your work, and will either
give you the same "let me know when you're in a showcase and
I'll try to get over to see it," or he'll ask to see "a piece of film."
That means, quite simply, he wants to see what you look like on
camera. He knows his business well enough to know that your
acting skills, live personality, and experience are less important
than your image on the screen, and he wants to find out what _that_
is before he spends time on you. He also knows that if he has some
film on you he can use it to sell you, because casting directors can
look at it and judge your quality and appropriateness for
themselves.

You contact an agent in Hollywood the same way as in New
York. Get a list of agents from the SAG office, send some photos
and a covering letter, and follow those up with phone calls. If you
can announce in your initial letter that you have "a piece of film,"
you will probably get an interview. Where do you get that film?
Try to do a film for some students at a film school. At N.Y.U. and
U.C.L.A. students are always seeking actors for their class pro-
jects. If the filmmaker apears to know what he's doing, if the
equipment being used might render a decent product, and if the
script is not excessively embarrassing you might exchange your
time and services for a print of the film. Another device is to
prepare a scene and then have it recorded on videotape. Many
colleges and universities now have nearly professional studios for
their students and a bit of sweet-talking can end with your
getting your scene taped. There are commercial firms that will
dub from tape to 16mm film—an electronic dubbing that loses one
"generation" of picture and sound quality, but which renders an

acceptable product if your original is first rate. Once you have your "piece of film" try to get an agent to screen it. He will commit himself on the basis of that screening.

All agents' contracts in Hollywood are "exclusive." Indeed, the standard contract ties up more than your acting talent. It will include all modeling, writing, and composing you do as well. While some agencies focus only on TV and film work, all have a working arrangement to handle commercials, and a commercials agent is employed by many large agencies. All these contracts have a time clause to them and if you find you've signed with an agent who is doing nothing for your career, you can move after a few months.

Which agent should you sign with? In most cases, the first one that offers. But you may wish to consider if a small or large agency is in your best interest. The small agency has fewer clients and may therefore work for you more often. However, it may not have as many contacts or as great a muscle in negotiations as the large agency. The large agency has so many clients that you might get lost in the shuffle, but it also is able to create "packages" for producers, supplying writers, directors, stars, and (yes) bright new talent for the small but choice role of.... It is not possible to weigh the pros and cons of the choices, but it is safe to say you will not have a choice at first and when you do you'll be experienced enough in the profession to make a wise one.

There are many jokes about agents and most are as cruel, as accurate, and as funny as the one told earlier about the boy who did bird imitations. The jokes result from actors' resentment of the fees paid to agents. That's an unfair resentment, if you consider how little the agent usually earns and what real services he does for you at contract time. Yet agents remain the butt of actors' frustrations. The actor wants to work, doesn't get work, and blames it on the agent who is "earning 10% for doing nothing." That's bad reasoning, of course, since the agent knows that 10% of nothing is nothing. But the out-of-work actor is impatient and the agent is a convenient scapegoat for his anger.

You will get along well with your agent if you keep in mind that he is a businessperson in a world peopled with arrogant, self-nominated artists. He is the voice of sound economics trying to moderate between a director whose producer can't afford to pay your fee and an actor who looks upon all businessmen as insensitive parasites. You might also remember that he will be more inclined to work for you if he likes you than if you condescend to him or if you nag him all the time. You might also remember that he knows as well as you that he is a middle man, a wholesaler, a dealer in your talents, and that he may be embarrassed by that truth. While he takes pride in doing his job well—negotiating a good contract, sending the right actor on the right audition, putting together the right package—he gets frustrated when he can't get work for his clients. You will get along well with him, and do yourself a good turn, if you will think of him not as the butt of a new joke but as a necessary and proper adjunct to your career.

Your Other Job

Acting is the hobby at which you spend 750 hours a year, right? What is the job you spend 1,250 hours a year doing? What do you do to earn a living while you make your rounds?

An actor's life requires flexibility and mobility in your non-theatre job. You've got to be able to take a morning off to attend an audition, take four weeks off to rehearse a play, and arrange a weekly schedule which permits you to attend classes and make the rounds. Not many employers will cooperate with you and those that will are likely to exploit you by paying poor hourly wages. But there are some jobs you can pursue.

The best of all is to be in the inheritance business. Get born into a family that can afford to support you during your initial years as an actor. If you have not had the foresight to arrange that, get someone to keep you. A husband or wife, a lover, or even a patron who fancies the notion of "owning" a struggling artist. Any source of income which leaves you entirely free to pursue your career is devoutly to be wished. Some young actors spend a couple of years working two jobs and saving a nest egg so they can come to New York or Hollywood with enough of a bankroll to last a year or more. That requires a great degree of self-discipline, but it can be preferable to arrangements which involve you unnecessarily with other people.

If you have to take a job, consider one on the swing shift. If you go to work at midnight and get off at eight in the morning, you can get a good sleep from nine to three in the afternoon and be up in time to make auditions and rounds in the late afternoon and classes in the early evening. Of course that throws your meal schedule into a tizzy and you can follow that upside-down schedule only if you live alone. If your roommate or spouse holds a day job and you pass each other in the hallway as you come and go, your relationship won't last a month. The swing shift solution is only for the solitary stalker with a flexible metabolism.

Another alternative is the type of hourly work suggested in the previous chapter: cab driver, bartender, waitress, clerk, telephone operator, etc. These are typical jobs for would-be actors and you'll find ads for positions in the trade papers. There are two problems with all such jobs. They don't pay much and they are dreary. If you are paid by the hour, and if you work an irregular schedule which totals only thirty hours a week, your pay packet will be a thin one. You probably won't be able to get along without dipping into your savings. Of all the part-time jobs, the best paying ones are in bars. Making and serving drinks is a big business in both New York and Hollywood, and if you are not disturbed by working in a lounge or pub, you'll bring home more money for less hours and retain a fair amount of flexibility in your schedule. But you need a strong sense of self to work at this kind of job for long.

The job you choose must not depress you, must not make you lose your love of the theatre. The theatre will bruise you enough. You'll lose out in auditions. You'll be in flops. You'll be rejected. You need some portion of your life that is cheery. You need to get up in the morning with something pleasant to look forward to—and that ought to be your non-theatre job. You ought to find a position which interests and challenges you, and in which you can take some pride.

There is a paradox here, of course. But the theatre never promised you a rose garden.

Unemployment Compensation

Most actors look upon unemployment compensation as a regular portion of their annual income. As our federal, state, and city governments are not very good about subsidizing the arts, many feel unemployment compensation is an indirect governmental subsidy of the artist.

The policies vary from state to state and are subject to change on short notice. A visit to the appropriate office will provide you with all the current information you need to file your claim. There are a couple of general rules which it might help you to know, however.

The unemployment office has the right to send you out on job interviews. If their files indicate you are a clerk-typist, you'll be obliged to go on any interviews they set up for you and to take any job you can't prove is unacceptable. To avoid this nuisance, make certain your job description is ACTOR. To do so, you must prove that your previous year's income was from acting. Don't go to file for the first time unless your previous year's reported earnings were 51% from acting.

Many theatre managements in states around New York will cooperate with you by paying you in New York and paying into the New York fund, so you can qualify for unemployment compensation when the job is completed. If you're being hired to work outside New York, check this out with the company manager and the unemployment office before you sign the contract.

Many states have reciprocal arrangements with New York and with each other. Since all these agreements are subject to alteration, check with your local office for accurate information and printed guidelines.

In New York, to qualify for benefits, you must have worked a minimum of 20 weeks during the previous fiscal year. You'll need to keep an accurate diary of your working weeks, as you may be able to negotiate with management to achieve that magic number 20. For instance, if you go on a stock job which will bring your total for the year to only 19 weeks, you might be able to arrange with the company manager to be paid for an extra week, with your final two weeks' salaries halved—thus bringing you the same gross you would otherwise have earned but stretching your total weeks of employment to the number required to qualify you for benefits. Or, you may choose between two stock jobs on the basis of the total weeks you'll work. If the difference will qualify you for 26 weeks your choice will be a clear one.

The unemployment office in Hollywood is one of the more amazing places you'll visit. The governances in California take into account that work in film and TV is irregular and short-lived. Accordingly, you can qualify for benefits if your gross earnings in the same fiscal quarter of the preceding year were above a specified figure, and if you are not working any given week at present. That means actors whose annual earnings are in the six figures can qualify for benefits any week they are not on a job. During my time in that line I stood next to several well-known actors. They command high salaries, have large annual incomes, and yet qualify for their weekly check. (If you have relatives who want to see a real, live movie star, tell them to go to the Hollyood unemployment office and they'll thank you forever afterwards.)

Taxes

You need a tax consultant. Even if your earnings are modest, you'll be astounded what a large refund a good tax consultant can arrange for you. Here is a partial list of the items you can legitimately deduct. Theatre tickets. Movie tickets. Business lunches. Postage. Photography. Printing of stationery and other materials related to your profession. Telephone and answering service charges. A percentage of per diem expenses for all the time you are on a job away from your home or residence. Makeup supplies. Theatrical wardrobe and maintenance. Scripts, scores, sheet music. Demo tapes and commercial prints. Trade advertisements. Classes, coaching, lessons. Records. The list is longer than I know or can recount.

Tax preparers charge in proportion to your gross income and you can find a reasonable one by chatting with other actors. Some are better than others, some more expensive than others, and some more pleasant than others. You'll have to do your own scouting around, but good tax people are well known, well respected, and easy to locate.

Don't knowingly break the law. With the aid and advice of a theatre-wise tax consultant you should find enough deductions to achieve a sizable annual refund without breaking the law.*

---

*See R. Brendan Hanlon, *A Guide to Taxes and Record Keeping for Performers, Directors, Designers* (New York: Drama Book Specialists [Publishers], 1978). —ED.

Going to the Theatre

When you go to the theatre you have obligations to the audience and to the players. You can make the theatre a rich and rewarding place to be, you can encourage audiences to return, and you can help the performers do their jobs if you will reflect in advance about your obligations and behave accordingly.

Today's audiences are reared on television, not live theatre. As a result they are prone to talk during the performance, rattle candy wrappers, and otherwise detract from the collective event. They do not *assist* in the event, as Peter Brook suggests they ought to in his concluding remarks in *The Empty Space*. They come only to watch as distanced observers and to be "entertained." You have the obligation to offer a model. You must behave as you want all audiences to behave.

You should dress appropriately. We are a society that respects uniforms. The policeman in plainclothes confuses us and the businessman who looks like a leather freak is unlikely to gain the respect of his peers. Audiences are no longer certain what uniform to wear to the theatre. As our society moves towards a pervasive casualness, the "sincere" suit is no longer appropriate, and the "basic" dress varies from region to region. The Broadway audience, the Hollywood audience, and the audience for the Actors Theatre of Louisville will dress differently. But all ought to dress in a manner which makes them feel they are participating in a friendly but significant event. You must judge the location and milieu of the theatre you're attending and offer yourself as a model for other audience members to observe. Then, next time, they may know how to dress, feel at home upon their arrival, and participate in the performance with confidence. In no way should your uniform announce that you are an actor. Don't be overly elegant to draw attention to yourself. Costume yourself as the character you are that night: Mr. Ideal Playgoer.

Be a supportive audience. Don't be absurdly disproportionate. Don't hoot and stamp your disapproval of an inept performance that the audience finds embarrassing and is polite enough to endure quietly, and don't guffaw like a jackass at some mildly amusing quip. And, worse, don't sit huddled inside yourself as though you were pretending to be somewhere else. The audience needs your laugh, your applause, and your presence.

Be polite, mature, and firm to those rude or ignorant people around you who are disturbing everyone. Today's audience is accustomed to talking during a TV program which is beamed into their bedroom and has no awareness that you and the performers might be bothered. They will probably shut up, if you let them know they are disruptive. If someone is talking, offer a subdued but authoritative, "Please do not talk!"

The performers need your assistance, also. Don't disrupt their work or distract their concentration by letting them know you are present. Try to select seats that aren't immediately visible from the stage, if you have acquaintances in the show. Don't tell people you're coming to the show, if you feel it would make them self-conscious to know you were watching. Don't go backstage before the show. They have enough to do to get their performance ready without having to deal with you.

Don't impose on your acquaintances for tickets. Tickets must always be purchased, and usually by the actor. Don't place friends in the awkward position of having to buy a ticket for you and then having to pretend it was complimentary. If your friend can get the stage manager to walk you in, fine. Otherwise, buy your ticket. When you're acting you can't afford to buy seats for all your acquaintances. Nor can they for you.

Always go backstage after a show. There will be many times when you will remain in your seat, having hated the show and the performances, and try to figure out what to say. It is easy to go back when you like something. But you must always go back. If you're hard-pressed for a comment, play at being a reporter. "The couple next to me loved it." "I overheard some woman at intermission tell her friend she was puzzled but absolutely wrapped up in the show." Ultimately your acquaintance will want to hear what you thought of him. No. He'll want to hear that you liked his work. So tell him. Lie, if need be. Later, some other month, you can be honest. For now, consider your obligation to the theatre. The audience deserves the best show it can get. The show will be best if the actors think they're doing it well. So serve the theatre now. And later serve the god of integrity.

Go backstage even if you don't know anyone in the show. Actors love to hear compliments from other actors, and you can help the performers and theatre (and yourself in the long run) if you will take a few minutes to say a kindly word or two to the actors who have just tried to do a good job. In this ego-riddled profession a flattering word from a fellow actor can off-set the most damaging review from some flippant journalist.

This Is Your Life

"Life upon the wicked stage ain't nothin' for a sweet, young girl," warns Oscar Hammerstein's lyric. And it ain't much for the guys either. It's a hard, frequently unrewarding, frustrating, and treacherous life, but it's the one you've chosen. You believe the rewards of fame or creative satisfaction will balance the payments you'll make in hard work and emotional self-sacrifice. Well, I hope for your sake that you're right. It is your life to live and if you want to dedicate it to Thalia, go right ahead. Just two final notions.

First. Your talent is singular, but the business of show business is a collective one. You will serve yourself best by serving the theatre best. The rules of the unions and the practices of the theatre are there to provide you with guidelines so that you and your fellow actors can thrive together in your common work. If the rules seem wrong, try to change them. But keep in mind that until such change comes about, you are well advised to respect and abide by those that exist. The theatre can give you much. You must give it its due, as well. The theatre is a very small world. Soon you'll know many of its citizens. Make certain you are a responsible citizen of that theatrical world yourself.

Second. You'll serve Thalia best by serving yourself. If you live your life richly, you'll help yourself to act with vitality and creative vibrance. You are the imitator of human action, and the more you know and experience of human activities, the more you will imitate with accuracy, specificity, economy, and passion. If you live a reclusive life, surrounded only with friends and artifacts of the theatre, you will not know enough of life to represent it. You must live a varied life. You owe it to yourself and your art to realize that you can behave well as an actor only by behaving well in life.

Be a political animal. Know something of the laws, government, and society you imitate in your work. You need not be a political activist carrying banners for candidates. You don't need to run for office yourself. Don't be so egotistical as to try parlaying your public's knowledge of your image into a quest for offices you're not qualified to perform. But you ought to be informed on issues. You ought to accept your obligations to vote and to serve on juries. You ought to be a citizen-actor. To hide behind a shield of artistic immunity is to do yourself and your world an unforgivable disservice.

Be culturally alert. Know what painters and composers are doing. Read the contemporary novelists. See the important new films. Read the newspapers and magazines which reflect your world.

Be a social creature. Know friends from many professions and economic classes. Don't limit your circle of friends to those who share your background and interests. Learn about life through the people you move among.

Travel. See new places, customs, cultures. Shed the deforming cloak of provincialism and don the enriching robes of inquiry.

"In the time of your life, live," wrote William Saroyan, "so that in that good time there shall be no ugliness or death for yourself or for any life your life touches. . . . In the time of your life, live— so that in that wondrous time you shall not add to the misery and sorrow of the world, but shall smile to the infinite delight and mystery of it."

Actor, this is your life. Live it so that you may act. Act so that you may be alive. Behave in your acting as you would behave in your life, for (and here comes the book's final maxim) *life is a continual rehearsal for a show that closes out of town.*